Louis Albert Banks

Paul and His Friends

A Series of Revival Sermons

Louis Albert Banks

Paul and His Friends
A Series of Revival Sermons

ISBN/EAN: 9783337116897

Printed in Europe, USA, Canada, Australia, Japan

Cover: Foto ©Lupo / pixelio.de

More available books at **www.hansebooks.com**

Paul and His Friends

A SERIES OF REVIVAL SERMONS

BY

Rev. LOUIS ALBERT BANKS, D.D.

PASTOR FIRST M. E. CHURCH, CLEVELAND, OHIO

AUTHOR OF

"Christ and His Friends," "The Fisherman and His Friends,"
"The Christian Gentleman," "Sermon Stories for
Boys and Girls," etc.

FUNK & WAGNALLS COMPANY

NEW YORK AND LONDON

COPYRIGHT, 1898, BY
FUNK & WAGNALLS COMPANY
[Registered at Stationers' Hall, London, England]
Printed in the United States of America

To

THE MEMBERS OF THE
FIRST METHODIST EPISCOPAL CHURCH
OF CLEVELAND, OHIO

WHOSE LOYAL SUPPORT MADE POSSIBLE THE GLORIOUS
REVIVAL IN THE WHITE HEAT OF WHICH
THESE SERMONS WERE FORGED
THIS VOLUME IS GRATEFULLY AND AFFECTIONATELY
DEDICATED BY THE AUTHOR

AUTHOR'S PREFACE.

The sermons contained in this volume were preached in the First Methodist Episcopal Church, Cleveland, Ohio, during the month of January, 1898, in a series of evangelistic meetings. The themes had been selected two years before and illustrations had been gathering during all that time; but each sermon was finally outlined and dictated to a stenographer on the day of delivery. One of the most gracious revivals I have ever known in my pastoral work accompanied their utterance. The blessing of God made them at that time a message of salvation to many hearts, and I pray for His continued blessing upon them as they go out in printed form. The other volumes of revival sermons which I have published have met with so wide a welcome in all parts of the English-speaking world that I am encouraged to hope that these discourses will bring suggestive and illustrative material to the hand of preachers, Sunday-school teachers, and soul-winners of every class.

Louis Albert Banks.

Cleveland, February 28, 1898.

CONTENTS.

	PAGE
A Motto for the New Year,	1
The Voice of God,	13
A Look Inside the Sky,	26
Kicking Against the Goad,	38
A Warm Hand-Grasp for the Man in the Dark,	48
A Man Who Failed Once, but Won on a Second Chance,	62
The Cure of Souls,	75
A Cry for Help from Silent Lips,	88
Gallio the Indifferent,	97
Burning the Bridges in the Rear,	110
The Fatal Blunder of a Shrewd Governor,	121
Obedience to the Heavenly Vision,	130
The Snare of the Soft South Winds,	140
The Emphatic Date in Human Life,	150
The Squandered Birthright,	160
The Lord's Brother,	169
The Greatest Thief in the World is Neglect,	182
A Friend Who Never Fails,	193

	PAGE
THE SWORD THAT CUTS BOTH WAYS,	202
THROWING THE SOUL'S PURSUERS OFF THE SCENT,	215
DRIFTING OUT OF THE TRACK OF THE HOME SHIPS,	224
THE INSPIRATION OF IMMORTALITY,	235
THE LORD'S SAINTS IN THE DEVIL'S PALACE,	245
THE STORY OF A SHIPWRECK,	258
CHRIST'S CONQUERING HEROES,	269
THE GREAT WRESTLING MATCH,	277
THE CREDENTIALS OF LOVE,	287
ESCAPE FROM A FATAL HANDICAP,	297
REAPING OUR OWN SOWING,	308
DESTINY DECIDED IN YOUTHFUL DAYS,	318
THE GREATEST SAYING IN THE WORLD,	327
THE WAITING CROWNS,	338

PAUL AND HIS FRIENDS.

A MOTTO FOR THE NEW YEAR.

"One thing I do, forgetting the things which are behind, and stretching forward to the things which are before, I press on toward the goal unto the prize of the high calling of God in Christ Jesus."—*Phil.* iii. 13, 14 (Rev. Ver.).

A MARVELOUSLY courageous Scripture is this, and one that ought to inspire our hearts in these last hours while we wait for the coming of the New Year. Paul evidently felt that there was no standstill to human life. He was a part of a great procession and must keep step with alert and eager tread. It will be well if we all catch his spirit, and can really sing with Mrs. Farningham:

"One by one, one by one,
 The years march past till the march is done;
 The Old Year dies to the solemn knell,
 And a merry peal from the clanging bell
 Ushers the others, one by one,
 Till the march of the years shall at last be done.

A MOTTO FOR THE NEW YEAR.

"Bright and glad, dark and sad,
  Are the years that come in mystery clad;
  Their faces are hidden, and none can see
  If merry or sorrowful each will be.
  Bright and sad, dark and glad,
  Have been the years that we all have had

"Fair and subtle under the sun,
  Something from us each year has won.
  Has it given us treasures? Day by day
  It has stolen something we prized away;
  We meet with fears, and count with tears,
  The buried hopes of the long past years.

"Is it so? And yet let us not forget
  How fairly the sun has risen and set;
  Each year has brought us some sunny hours,
  With a wealth of song and a crown of flowers.
  Power to love, and time to pray,
  Its gifts have been ere it passed away.

"We hail the New Year that has come in view;
  Work comes with it, and pleasure too;
  And even tho it may bring some pain,
  Each passing year is a thing of gain;
  We greet with song the days that throng.
  Do they bring us trouble? 'Twill make us strong.

"With smiles of hope and not with tears,
  We meet our friends in the glad New Years;
  God is with them, and as they come,
  They bear us nearer our restful home;
  And one by one, with some treasure won,
  They come to our hearts till they all are gone."

The Scriptures have so many appeals intended to arouse us to be alert and wakeful as to our duty, and there are so many calls to remembrance that we are startled, almost, to have the wide-awake Paul come to us with an appeal for forgetfulness, and yet such it is. He declares that a part of the preparation he makes for future victory is forgetfulness of the things which are behind.

Of course Paul does not mean that he will forget the things of the past that are comforting to his heart, and tend to establish his faith and make him stronger as a friend and servant of Christ. What he means is that he will not allow anything that may have happened in his past to hover about him like a ghost and cause his spirit to be less courageous for the work he has in hand to do. No past event shall hang as a millstone about his neck to hinder him in his Christian course. And in that we should imitate him.

One night at bedtime a little child begged for the story of Daniel.

"I am afraid," said the mother, "if I tell you the story, you will dream about the lions."

"Oh, no," returned the little one, "I will dream about Daniel and leave out the lions."

We should do that with our past. We should get all the courage we can from it, but yet let no roaring lions that may be in it prevent us from taking advantage of the new opportunities which are ours to-day.

There are two kinds of things we ought to forget in order to do our best in the new year. First, we ought to forget our failures. Not that we shall not learn by experience; if we gain wisdom by noting where we might have acted differently, and have thus changed defeat into victory, retrospection is a good thing; but we should not for a moment treasure up the memory of a failure in the past as any sort of an indication that we are going to fail this year. Let us forget past failures, and, remembering the infinite love and mercy of God, assured of the presence of the Holy Spirit, here and now, knowing that Christ is here to enter the New Year with us, and that through him we can do all things, let us go forth to battle and to victory as tho there never had been a failure in our lives.

On the other hand, if we are to do our best work in the year to come, it is just as necessary that we forget our past successes. People who live on their record never amount to much. The dead-line runs through that hour of a man's life in which he is satisfied with himself and looks with self-complacency on what he has accomplished. It is the hungering, thirsting soul for which there is waiting a still greater abundance. It is the stretching-forward people, who see prizes yet aloft in the sky, who work wonders in the world. There is no dead-line for anybody for whom the future holds more intense struggles than the past.

This is a very critical point for every one of us. If we enter upon this series of meetings with a sort of self-satisfaction, and expect to feel complacent at the end whether through God's grace we win souls or not, then we shall not be of much value in this great campaign which we open to-night in the name of Jesus Christ our Lord. But if it seems to each of us—as it ought, no matter what our past successes as soul-winners may have been—that, compared with the tender love of Christ for us and in the light of his infinite sacrifice on our behalf, what we have done hitherto is very small and insignificant, and if there is in our hearts a great longing to win poor sinners to know the riches of the forgiveness of sins which we have found ourselves, then there is hope that Christ may be able to use us to his honor and glory.

Exceedingly interesting and forceful is this splendid figure which Paul uses to indicate the intensity with which he is determined to pursue the Christian life. You will notice that it is a stronger figure than that presented in the Old Version. There it is "reaching forth." Well, a man may reach forth while he remains standing, and without changing the position of his body, except the arm and hand; but "stretching forward" suggests something into which the whole man enters. It is the figure of the athlete, the stretching eager body of the runner with eye on the prize. It gives one the impression of a whole-souled earnestness, and that above everything else is what we need on the human side in our great work of winning men and women to Christ. Ordinary abilities become charged with marvelous power when a man throws his whole heart and soul into the service of God so that the Holy Spirit illuminates his common gifts and makes them glorious and efficient. The only difference between a bit of black carbon and a luminous lamp that makes the street bright as day at midnight is in the electricity which passes through the carbon. Often the only difference between two church-members of equal gifts and opportunities, the one constantly winning souls to Christ and doing helpful service for the Lord while the other seems only a respectable idler in the outer kingdom, is that one is like the dead carbon—moral, respectable, upright, but with no light or fire or power—and the other is so given over to God that the electricity of the Holy Spirit shines through word and face and deed until the words of Christ are realized again, "Ye are the light of the world."

This leads us to another striking figure used in our text—the word "press." Paul says: "I press on toward the goal." You know at once where was the chief emphasis of Paul's life. The thing a man cares for most is the thing he presses. In this modern complex life of ours we are many-sided; we are variously related to society and to business. It can not be said of any one of us that we are simply one thing, and yet there is some one point where we put the emphasis. A business man has many investments, but there is some one business that either on account of his taste, or through the promise of speedy or great returns, he is most interested in, and he so presses that one thing that whenever you think of him it is in connection with that one business, because there is the chief emphasis of his business life. Now I take it that Paul felt that it was his highest duty and privilege to put the great emphasis of life on the fact that he was the friend and servant of Jesus Christ. Incidentally Paul did other things. He had been a law student; he knew how to make tents—sometimes worked at it for years at a time after he was a minister; he was a good friend; for that day, he was a great traveler. But so tremendously did Paul put the emphasis of his life on this one thing that I imagine whenever a member of the Jewish Sanhedrin, or a business man of

Ephesus, or a Roman soldier, or a politician spoke of Paul, it was as "Paul the Christian." Let us ask ourselves very earnestly to-night: "Where am I putting the emphasis of my life? On business? On politics? On circles of pleasure? On social competitions? Where?" It is a very important query. Do not thrust it aside.

There can be no doubt where the emphasis ought to be. It ought to be with us, as with Paul, that the point where we press hardest is toward the great goal of fulfilling our duty to Christ. If we are not doing that, if money-making comes first, and so far first that our Christianity is a poor second, we ought to repent before God this very hour. If pleasure, or social success, or personal pride, or self-indulgence of any kind, is the thing of first importance with us, so that loving worship and service for Christ is almost distanced in the race, then God pity us, and arouse us out of the slumber that threatens us with eternal disaster!

And now, one thing more. "One thing I do," says the apostle. Are we ready to say that for the next month? Incidentally we shall have to do other things. We shall have to cook and eat and drink as usual; most of you will have to go about your regular work of life. But it is possible that a great overmastering purpose may so enter into us and possess us that whether about our work, or at our meals, or in our daily meeting with our fellows, we shall still be doing only *one thing*. The one thing I call you to is the salvation of souls. It is the greatest thing in the world. Some one inquired of Dr. Lyman Beecher in his old age: "Doctor, you have lived a long time, and seen and known many things; what do you consider the main thing?" The grand old hero of twoscore and more revivals answered without a moment's hesitation, "It is not theology; it is not controversy; it is *saving souls*."

God help us to believe that to our finger-tips! Let us believe it so thoroughly that we shall be willing to do anything, however insignificant or humble it may seem, that may help to bring about the revival of God's grace in our hearts. People that are thoroughly mastered by their purpose are not oversensitive or particular where they are put to work.

A few years after the war military titles were very cheap and common. A story is told of an old farmer who had a considerable number of men at work in his hay-field. A traveler, stopping to converse with the farmer, was interested in the latter's remark that most of his men were old soldiers.

"Indeed! Are any of them officers?"

"Two of them. One of them over there was a private, and that fellow beyond was a corporal;

but the man beyond him was a major, and that man away over in the corner was a colonel."

"Indeed! Are they good men?"

"Well," said the farmer, "that private is a first-class man, and the corporal is pretty good, too."

"But how about the major and the colonel?"

"The major's so-so," said the farmer.

"But the colonel?"

"Well," answered the farmer, "I ain't a-going to say a word against a man who was a colonel in the war, but I've made up my mind to one thing—I ain't a-going to hire any brigadier-generals!"

God give us such supreme love for Christ, such a longing to win our neighbors to know the good things that await them in the Gospel, that we shall be ready to fall into the ranks anywhere where we may give, it may be, only "a cup of cold water" in his name. Don't think you can do nothing because you do not seem to be specially gifted. Every one of us can pray, and prayer is our greatest weapon.

A young man was saved on his dying bed. Once saved he began to think of his companions, thoughtless young fellows just such as he was before he was led to see that he needed a Savior. He asked his pastor what he should do for them. The pastor bade him pray for them and put their names upon a card so that he might not forget any one of them. This the sick man did, and his death-chamber was hallowed by his many prayers. He died, and soon after his death the church over which his pastor ministered was revived. During the revival every one of the young men so earnestly prayed for was converted.

If every one of us shall press forward earnestly to do this *one thing*, then the conditions of Pentecost will be met again, and night after night we shall be with *one accord* in *one place*, and the saving mercy of God will come upon the people.

Let us see to it that this "accord" be not broken by lack of harmony. Webster says that "accord" means "agreement in pitch and tone." You may have a hundred singers, or a hundred instruments of music, but if three or four of them are out of pitch and tone there will be discord instead of harmony. Let the prayer of each one be, "God save me from being the discordant note that shall render powerless the love and faith and service of all the rest!"

A great concert can only be brought about by a great deal of individual practise on the part of the musicians. Each one must come from many private rehearsals prepared to do his own work. So in the secret closet, where we open our hearts to God in confession and repentance and faith, we must prepare ourselves so that when we come together in the house of God it will not be the bringing together of dry bones, or dead brands, but the bringing together of living souls, of burning spirits, of hearts illuminated by the Holy Spirit. On such a meeting the gift of tongues will come again. No man or woman or child will come into this place without feeling that in deed and in truth they have heard the Gospel in their own tongue, and the old cry of Pentecost, "What must we do to be saved?" will gladden our hearts, and cause all the bells of heaven to ring for joy.

THE VOICE OF GOD.

"God, having of old time spoken unto the fathers in the prophets by divers portions and in divers manners, hath at the end of these days spoken unto us in his son."—*Heb.* i. 1, 2 (Rev. Ver.).

GOD has never ceased to speak to mankind. He spoke to Adam and Eve in the Garden of Eden face to face. He came to Abraham in the desert in the form of an angel. He spoke to Moses on Mount Horeb from the flames of the burning bush, and on Mount Sinai from the enveloping clouds. He spoke to Elijah in the roar of the wind, the crash of the thunder, and "the still, small voice." He spoke to Joseph and Daniel and Ezekiel in dreams and visions. For hundreds of years he spoke to the people through the mouth of his prophets. Elijah and Elisha, Isaiah, Jeremiah, Daniel and Hosea, Jonah and Habakkuk, Joel and Amos and their compeers, were the voices of God crying aloud his message.

All these great personalities were also the heralds to make way for the coming of Christ, by whom God is speaking unto us to-day. Every one of the prophets looking down through the mist of the distant years saw with more or less clearness the coming of the Son of God who was also to be the Son of man. At last, in the fulness of time, Christ came in the fulfilment of prophecy. Jesus himself declares that the Old-Testament Scriptures are fulfilled in him. The whole Bible, Old and New Testaments taken together, might be compared to the progress of a single day. The sunrise would be in Genesis, with its early twilight of creation and its rays of divine hope in the promises of God to Abraham. The morning advances through the times of the patriarchs, the wanderings in the wilderness, and the entrance to the promised land. The sun climbs high in the heavens in the songs of David and in the splendid vision of the Savior in the chapters of Isaiah, all pointing to the high-noontide of revelation in the person of Jesus Christ. On through the advancing hours of the glorious afternoon we turn through the matchless letters of Paul and the heart-searching epistles of Peter and James and John, till we reach the sunset hour of the vision from Patmos in the book of Revelation.

The Bible is a whole. You can not carve it in pieces and take out here and there a section to suit your taste or inclination. You can not have noon and evening without morning. There was never yet a sunset without a sunrise. Blot out the Old Testament and the New Testament is untranslatable; but keep both together and it is the simple story of God's conversations with his children, and a wayfaring man tho a fool need not err therein. Jesus fully recognized the Old Testament. He put his divine seal on all the twilight and morning of Scripture record and prophecy. The servant is not greater than his Lord. Let us cling to the blessed old Book. As Joseph Choate, the great lawyer, said at Dr. Storrs's anniversary: "If we can have only one book left, let us cling to that." Dr. Watkinson said, in speaking at the last General Methodist Conference, that when he was in Cologne he looked into that great cathedral. When he went in the early morning he saw that the eastern window was lighted up and all the other windows were dark and obscure. When he went at noon he found that some of the other windows had turned to ruby and gold, and that they flamed out in prophets, in angels, and saints. And then, when he went at sunset, he saw that the other windows were lighted up by the setting sun. And those that looked black in the morning, at night were illuminated and glorified until they looked like windows into heaven. It is a good deal like that, declared the great preacher, with the Bible. There are dark pages in it, but in the process of the sun first one page is lighted up and then another, and where men could see only obscurity there flames out magnificent meaning, with Jesus Christ always standing in the midst. There was truth for Chrysostom's day; truth for Bernard's; truth for Luther's; truth for Wesley's; and we of to-day are finding the exact truth for our particular generation and the singular condition of things in which we find ourselves. And before this world is done, there won't be a dark page left in the Book, but every bit of it will be illuminated, and the temple filled with the glory of God and with the gladness of men.

God is still speaking to us through his Son. When Jesus was on earth he held converse with his disciples face to face and spoke to wayside acquaintances and multitudes of strangers with the greatest simplicity and directness. But as the time for his great sacrifice of himself as a sin-offering for the guilt of the world drew near, he assured his disciples that after his departure he would send the Holy Spirit, not only to comfort them, but to bear witness of him and to bring his words to the remembrance of human hearts. We live in the days of the Holy Spirit, and Jesus Christ is speaking to us through him. The Holy Spirit has many ways of bringing the words of

Christ to our remembrance so that they shall give us comfort.

A recent writer tells of a friend who lately received in a dream just such a message as our calm thought tells us might well be the comfort that all our loved ones who have gone on before us into heaven would whisper in our ears could we but hear them. This friend had lost, by sudden death, one that was very dear to him, a friend and pupil, a sweet Christian boy. The bereavement weighed heavily upon his heart for many days. A week or two after the funeral he had a dream. He dreamed that he sat by his desk in his study, and Steve (that was the young pupil's name) entered the door. His appearance did not startle him; for altho he was conscious that he had died, yet it seemed perfectly natural for him to come to see him again. He advanced across the room, and stood between his teacher's knees, close up to his chair, placing his hands upon the man's shoulders and looking into his face. Nothing was said for a time, and then the teacher burst out weeping. After a moment he said to the boy, "Oh, Steve, I would give everything, all that I possess in this world, if I could only have you back again." The pupil leaned over, folding his arms about his teacher's neck, and resting his head upon the older man's shoulder, and said very earnestly and tenderly, yet with almost a reproof in his tones: "Oh no! no! no! you don't understand; you don't understand." That was all. But the good man woke up happy, and with more spiritual insight and comfort than he had had since the boy's death. He felt that all was well, and that his sorrow was all of ignorance, and that some time he would understand.

But such visions as that do not come to unprepared hearts. It is only a heart softened and mellowed by the showers of divine grace and instructed in the hope of the Gospel that is so fitted that the Holy Spirit can thus comfort it. The Holy Spirit uses the promises of God's Word and the words of Christ for the salvation of men. If this be true, how important it is that we should make ourselves acquainted with the Word of God, and with the life and teachings of Jesus, so that we shall be susceptible to the impressions of the Holy Spirit. I fear that the very helpfulness of the Sunday-school has led parents in our time to make the great blunder of depending almost entirely upon it as the moral and religious teacher of their children. However good the Sunday-school may be, there never was a Sunday-school yet so rich in Bible instruction and moral and religious teaching as to make it sufficient to take the place of daily religious teaching on the part of father and mother in the home.

Dr. Hillis, of Chicago, declares that for more than a generation parents have been farming out their children for moral training. The time was when the youth of the country were trained primarily at home, and only incidentally in the Sunday-school. But the time has come when the moral instruction of the children is confined to a brief half-hour upon one day in seven. In the old days the parents rose up early, and trained the child to commit to memory not simply a golden text, but whole chapters of the Bible; not to read a lesson leaf, but a book, bearing upon the theme. The college professors and presidents, the statesmen and preachers, the men who have molded society during the past generation, received in Christian homes patient, thorough, and long-continued Bible instruction. Daniel Webster used to say that his standard of oratorical excellence was derived from such Scriptures as the eighth Psalm and the fortieth chapter of Isaiah. Carlyle said that he owed everything to the thorough mastery of about a hundred chapters in the Bible. Ruskin declares that his beautiful diction is traceable to the fact that his mother required him to commit to memory whole chapters of the New Testament, and many chapters of Moses, David, and Isaiah. "But in the stress and haste of modern life the religious instruction of children has sadly suffered. In the morning, business men have not time for the moral training of their children. In the evening they have no strength. On Sunday they excuse themselves on the ground that they leave ethics and religion to the Sunday-school." But we must all confess, after we have given the Sunday-school its highest meed of praise, that it is entirely insufficient to take the place of that quiet, personal, heart-searching conversation concerning spiritual things which some of us remember, and will remember until we stand in judgment before God, as hours of spiritual vision when father or mother talked to us before the open Bible in our own childhood.

Let us not make the fatal mistake of being less careful of the moral and spiritual education of our children than we are of their physical and intellectual training. We personally see to it that they have good food for their bodies, and if they do not have appetite for it, or take sufficient of such nourishment, the physician responds to our anxious call. But multitudes of children who are thus kindly and carefully looked after in physical matters are left to be little better than spiritual orphans.

Parents leave their children thus untaught and

untrained in God's Word, and then wonder why it is that the Holy Spirit does not speak to their children's hearts with such power as to win them to salvation. The Holy Spirit will take advantage of any seed of divine truth which he finds in our hearts. Jesus was ever doing that when he was here on earth. Take, as an example, the poor, wicked woman at the well in Samaria. Sinful tho she was, she was well instructed in the religion of her fathers. She knew the differences in the belief of the Jews and Samaritans, and had studied the prophecies concerning the coming of the Messiah. It was that early teaching that made it possible for Jesus to find his way to the secret places of her heart. He discovered what no one else had dreamed of, that hidden away under all her sinful life were fine feelings, serious thoughts, deep longings for better living, tho they would have all amounted to nothing if she had not met Jesus. But when Christ came these hidden seeds of truth, stowed away it may have been by a loving mother, were brought to light by him, and her desert life blossomed as the rose; and instead of the thorn of worldliness came up the fir-tree of faith, and instead of the briar of disobedience came up the myrtle-tree of obedience and love. God help us to plant in the minds and hearts of our children the Word of

God which may be used by the Holy Spirit unto their salvation!

But no doubt I am speaking to many who have been taught in God's Word and to whom God has spoken by the Holy Spirit, convicting you of sin, of righteousness, and of judgment, and yet you have closed your ears against the voice of God and refused him your obedience.

Perhaps some one replies, "The way of salvation does not appeal to my reason, and there are so many things commanded that seem unnecessary to me. I can not understand how the soul may be uplifted and saved in that way."

The Scripture declares, "Obedience is better than sacrifice." When Nicodemus could not understand even the first principles of spiritual things, Jesus said to him that as "the wind bloweth where it listeth, and thou hearest the sound thereof, but canst not tell whence it cometh nor whither it goeth, so is every one that is born of the Spirit."

Obey the voice of God. Yield your heart to the Lord Jesus. Turn away from your sins, ceasing to do them, and confess Jesus as your Savior and King. Light will fall upon your path, and glorious rewards will come to you as you obey him.

The story is told of an Eastern king who was once in need of a faithful servant and friend. He gave notice that he wanted a man to do a day's work, and two men came and asked to be employed. He engaged them both for certain fixed wages, and set them to work to fill a basket with water from a neighboring well, saying he would come in the evening and see their work. He then left them to themselves and went away. After putting in one or two bucketfuls one of the men said:

"What is the good of doing this useless work? As soon as you put the water in on one side, it runs out on the other."

The other man answered: "But we have our day's wages, haven't we? The use of the work is the master's business, not ours."

"I am not going to do such fool's work," replied the other; and throwing down his bucket he went away.

The other man continued his work till about sunset, when he exhausted the well. Looking down into it, he saw something shining at the bottom. Carefully letting down his bucket once more, he drew up a precious diamond ring.

"Now I see the use of pouring the water into a basket," he exclaimed to himself. "If the bucket had brought up the ring before the well was dry, it would have been found in the basket. The labor was not useless after all."

But he had yet to learn why the king had ordered

this apparently useless task. It was to test their capacity for perfect obedience, without which no servant is reliable. At this moment the king came up to him; and, as he bade the man keep the ring, he said: "Thou hast been faithful in a little thing; now I see I can trust thee in great things. Henceforth thou shall stand at my right hand."

Shall you not be as wise as that servant? How many witnesses you have to the wisdom and goodness and loving purpose of our King, Jesus Christ! Nothing but good and blessing can possibly come to you by obediently answering to his call.

It is possible that some are hearing the invitation for the last time.

One Sabbath evening some years ago, at the Methodist church in Hempstead, Long Island, the pastor conducted a short after-meeting. He sang two verses of "The Sweet By-and-By" very tenderly and effectively.

After the service an old gentleman came up to the pastor and said: "If you will sing the hymn 'The Sweet By-and-By' next Sabbath evening, I will be here."

The pastor willingly gave the promise.

The next Sunday evening a similar service was held after the regular evening service. The pastor told the people present that at the request of a gentleman present he would sing again the hymn

"The Sweet By-and-By." After the hymn had been sung an invitation for all those who wished to give their hearts to Christ was given. The pastor said to the old gentleman: "And won't you, too, accept the invitation to go forward?"

The old man yielded to this appeal, and after a season of prayer in which he found the Lord to the joy of his soul, the pastor inquired his name.

The reply was, "Joseph Hooker." It was none other than the hero of Lookout Mountain.

He was asked if he would come to the regular church prayer-meeting on Friday night to relate his experience, and to tell to others what a dear Savior he had found. He consented, but on the Tuesday evening following he fell dead from heart disease. He had heard the last invitation, and, thank God! he had accepted it.

To-day is the day of salvation. If ye hear his voice, harden not your hearts.

A LOOK INSIDE THE SKY.

"Behold I see the heavens opened, and the Son of man standing on the right hand of God."—*Acts* vii. 56 (Rev. Ver.).

STEPHEN's term of service as an official representative of Jesus was not long, as men count time, but so perfect was his fidelity, so intense his devotion, so radiant his life with the spirit of his Master, that it burned for him a large and brilliant circle in the memory of the church. Stephen is one of the few Scripture characters about whom there are no regrets. There is no period of early persecution like Paul's, no flame of anger as in John's case, no days of gloomy doubt and unbelief as with Thomas, no sudden cowardice and denial as in the experience of Peter. Here is a lamp that burned clear—a nature so completely given up to God, a soul so enraptured with Jesus Christ, a personality so devoted to the bidding of the divine will, that no self-interest or stain or tarnish of sin remained to dim the luster of the heavenly light shining through. If we would be triumphant Christians, irresistible in the wisdom and spirit with which we carry on our battles for the Master, there can be no better subject for our study. Altho Stephen was chosen not to be a minister, but a lay-worker, in the early church, he set about his work with such interest and enthusiasm that he was at once surrounded with people whose wicked hearts made them bitterly opposed to the new gospel of love and purity of which he was so shining an example. Altho we have no reason to believe that Stephen had been in public life in any way before or had had any experience as a public teacher, he was so full of faith, and so bright and clear in his Christian experience, and his heart so glowed with the presence of the Holy Spirit, that his opponents soon found that they had met more than their match, for, as the record says, "They were not able to withstand the wisdom and spirit by which he spake."

It is this clearness of faith, this vital Christian experience, this wisdom from heaven, this spirit of the ever-living God, which alone can make us conquering Christians in our own day. We may have our splendid churches, beautiful and well appointed; we may have our music which will charm the ear and delight the heart; we may have eloquence in the pulpit, and culture and respectability in the pews; but all will be in vain in fulfilling the great purpose for which the church exists, unless the divine magnetism of that heavenly atmosphere which Stephen breathed is vitally present in our hearts and lives. All signs of earthly prosperity on the part of the church are a miserable and insufficient apology for the lack of the life of God. Any mere pride of church success, or enthusiasm for church leadership, is a painted fire compared to the fire of the Holy Ghost which ought to flame first on the altars of our individual hearts, and then flame forth in mighty conflagration in the house of God. As another has well said, our manufactured "waters" are miserable mockeries if substituted for Heaven's River of the Water of Life. Our dainty confections can never take the place of God's wholesome bread. It is life of which our nerves are scant, more life and fuller life that we need, and which God is so willing to bestow.

Events matured quickly in Stephen's experience. His enemies, unable to answer him, sought to obtain revenge by bringing him before the Council, and there, by bribed witnesses, they swore away his life. But on Stephen's part there was no hesitation. He saw the clouds gathering, and must have known there could be but one end to that storm of wickedness and wrath; but in the midst of the bigotry and cruelty that surrounded him, even his enemies who sat in the Council and heard his wonderful plea for his Savior and his Lord, "fastening their eyes on him, saw his face as it had been the face of an angel."

Stephen was the man with the shining face. Luke, who writes the account, does not take time to tell us of the life behind that face, except as is indicated in the brief description of his character: "a man full of faith and of the Holy Spirit." But we know that back of that wisdom and irresistible moral force, back of that shining face, there was a hidden life of faith and prayer and communion with God. The quantity of our spiritual power is measured by the reservoir of the life-force that is "hid with Christ in God." Great spiritual battles are first fought and won in the secret chambers of the soul, in the closet of prayer, where the struggler wrestles with God as Jacob did with the angel at the old Jabbok ford. Luther unchained the Bible first in his study where his soul found the freedom of faith. Methodism and its revolution for righteousness had its first victory in Susannah Wesley's family prayers, and its next triumph in the little Holy Club at Oxford. There can be no victorious outward life in spiritual things except there first be the inward conquest. How clearly this is illustrated in the life of Jesus! Even the divine Savior felt the need of preparing for his public work of helpfulness and salvation by feeding in quiet those unseen forces which glorified him before the multitude. He sought seasons of solitude, hours of silence, when his great soul gave itself up to meditation and intense communion with God. If this is true of our Master, how much more certain is our need of increasing the hidden supply upon which we may draw when we come in contact with those who know not Christ. If we are to have the shining face we must have the glowing heart ever filled with heavenly light. For what lives and glows in our heart's inner recesses will make itself known in our outward deeds.

A gentleman of France, who had been delighted with the rapturous warblings of the nightingales of the forests of Sierra Morena, greatly desired to hear in the forests of his own estate the same entrancing music. No nightingale had ever been seen or heard within his woods, but he set himself to woo their presence. He reasoned that if he should make his grounds perfectly adapted to the comfort and happiness of nightingales, the unknown messengers of nature would in some way carry the news to the sweet singers and they would come. He undertook to make a perfect home for nightingales, and trusted nature to do the rest. Accordingly he banished cats and hawks and screech-owls, for the nightingale nests low and sings long, and is an easy prey to all these enemies of birds. He caused many places in the woods to be scratched up and had a kind of earth-worms of which nightingales are peculiarly fond planted liberally in accessible spots. He searched the literature of the world on the subject of nightingales and their habits, and every suggestion that pointed toward making a paradise for nightingales was at once put into practise. He waited a whole year, and not a note from a nightingale fell upon his ear. Another year passed by, and tho the preparations for their comfort went on unceasingly, the invited guests remained aloof. But when the third springtime came, one night, as the shadows were darkening, his ear was delighted and his heart thrilled with the song of the nightingale. A single pair of birds had found their way to that choice retreat. But they were only the pioneers of multitudes that were to follow them. Before many springs had passed his woods were so vocal with the songs of these famous birds that his estate was known far and wide as the "Garden of the Nightingales."

Shall we not learn the sweet and beautiful lesson? If nightingales of tenderness, larks of joy, holy doves of peace are to sing in our hearts and make our lives vocal with heavenly music, it must be because every vicious lust and preying appetite and lurking passion of evil has been banished from the soul. Only a nature given up to be the garden of God, prepared by faith and prayer for his coming, can be filled by the Christian graces. We can not have Stephen's power without Stephen's purity and consecration. But, thank God! they are both possible to us. The same divine Lord who had made conquest of his soul, whose loving presence as a sacred guest in his heart gave him his shining face, is seeking to dwell in our hearts and bestow upon us all spiritual charms.

To Stephen the heavens opened and he saw not only the glory of God, but his enraptured vision feasted most of all on his blessed Savior, whom he beheld "standing on the right hand of God." We do not come to a stern monarch with our plea for mercy and help, but to a tender-hearted heavenly Father whose glory is in no way displayed so magnificently as in his pity and compassion. The atonement was not the cause of God's love, but his love was the cause of the atonement. "God so loved the world that he gave his only-begotten Son, that whosoever believeth in him should not perish, but have eternal life."

Some of you may remember the beautiful pathos of Coventry Patmore's poem. He had found it necessary to discipline his little motherless boy and send him to bed. But it hurt him more than it did the child, as every true father or mother can understand, and after a while he could endure the soreness of heart no longer and went to see the child. He found him asleep, with all the queer things that fill a little boy's pocket set out beside him. In his grief the little fellow had comforted his soul with these trinkets, and had fallen asleep in peace. The father writes:

> "So when that night I pray'd
>   To God, I wept, and said:
>   ' Ah, when at last we lie with trancèd breath,
>   Not vexing thee in death;
>   And thou rememberest of what toys
>   We made our joys,
>   How weakly understood
>   Thy great commanded good,
>   Then, fatherly not less
>   Than I whom thou has molded from the clay,
>   Thou'lt leave thy wrath, and say,
>   "I will be sorry for their childishness." ' "

That melts us with its tender humanness, but there is something deeper and tenderer in these words of God through the mouth of his prophet: "I, even I, am he that blotteth out thy transgressions . . . and will not remember thy sins."

But there is a still deeper note in the suggestion of Stephen's vision of Jesus at the right hand of God, standing there in fulfilment of the precious promise that when he arose from the grave and passed into the heavens he would become our High

Priest and Intercessor before the throne of God. Before the Savior went away from his disciples he told them, to comfort them in their loneliness, that whatever they should ask in his name, that was good enough to be given, should be granted unto them. That promise has never been revoked and is true for us to-day. Our heavenly Father can not deny or refuse the intercession of him who was rich, and yet for our sakes became poor. We should never let the deep tenderness and pathos of those blessed words with which we close our prayers, "For Jesus's sake," be lost out of our affectionate appreciation.

A London cabman, who was a noble Christian man, came whirling around the corner into a side street, when a daring little lad ran recklessly in front of his horses. There was only one way to save the child, and that was to bring the horses to their haunches and to swing them to one side so quick that the driver was thrown to the curbstone, where he lay bleeding and dying.

They picked him up tenderly and took him to the hospital, and sent for his wife. As she sat by him in her quiet grief, the nurse inquired: "Have you any children?"

This question brought a fresh burst of tears. "We had one, little Teddy, but he is dead. My husband never rightly got over the loss of our only boy."

When at midnight he became conscious, his first question was, "Was the little fellow hurt?"

"No, the children are all safe; it is you who are hurt."

"Thank God! thank God!"

His wife bending over him, said: "But I am afraid you have killed yourself, Tom."

"Yes, but it was for little Teddy's sake. It was a near toucher, tho. A little boy with blue eyes, just like Teddy's, was making straight for the horses. I should have been over him in a moment! Ah, how glad I am I didn't!"

If God has made the heart of a London cabman so large that "for little Teddy's sake," whose blue eyes had been long since closed in death, he could gladly give his own life to save from harm a little stranger child, with what confidence and boldness ought we to come to the mercy-seat and ask forgiveness and help of him who has bidden us ask what we will in the name of his Son who died on the cruel cross for us.

No wonder that with such a vision rejoicing his heart, Stephen fell asleep with tender prayers for his enemies and rapturous hope for himself. The stones of his slayers were changed to jewels in his crown. There was no loneliness about such a death, for heaven's court opened to receive him, and his Lord was there to give him welcome. He who had said to his disciples only a little while before, "If I go and prepare a place for you, I will come again and receive you unto myself," had kept his promise and was at the trysting-place to meet his faithful friend. How blessed, how victorious, such a death!

But death without Christ is lonely indeed. The chaplain of the Pennsylvania state prison once related to a friend that one of the most pitiful of the tragic sights he had seen there was the death of a big, burly young fellow who was serving out a term of ten years.

One day, when the man had been suffering terrible agony from his disease, he suddenly asked: "Is there any hope for me?"

The doctor, after a moment's hesitation, shook his head.

"How long?"

"But a brief time."

From his pallet he could look through the grated window on a patch of dark sky. He stared at it and then cried out: "I can't! I can't go out there alone! God is waiting."

The chaplain told him God was merciful; but his heart had been hardened against the Holy Spirit so long that he would not listen, and cried out: "Not alone! I can't go alone! Is nobody else dying in the jail? Send for my old father. He'll be glad to die with me."

The chaplain told him of Christ and his love, but the ears of his spiritual understanding were deaf, and even when his breath was almost gone, he muttered again and again, "I can't face God alone!"

His father was sent for. He was an old man, near to the grave. He would gladly have died for the boy who had so darkened his own life; but he could only stand helpless beside the chaplain, listening to his son's moans of terror.

At last the strong body lay still. The soul, terror-stricken, full of horror in the face of deserved punishment, dreading above all else to meet the God against whom he had sinned, had gone out alone to meet its Maker.

What a contrast to this sad picture is the victorious translation of Stephen! Stephen, too, was conscious that God was waiting for him, but with delight, not terror, did he go forth to meet him. There was no sense of loneliness, for Christ was there to give him loving welcome. Surely every one of us is ready to cry out with Balaam: "Let me die the death of the righteous, and let my last end be like his."

KICKING AGAINST THE GOAD.

"Saul, Saul, why persecutest thou me? It is hard for thee to kick against the goad. And I said, Who art thou, Lord? And the Lord said, I am Jesus whom thou persecutest."—*Acts* xxvi. 14, 15 (Rev. Ver.).

EVERYTHING conspires to make the conversion of St. Paul one of the most striking and vivid pictures in the history of mankind. The keenness of his mind, his logical temperament, the thoroughness of his intellectual training, the intensity of his early prejudice against Christianity, his conspicuous career as a persecutor of the new faith—all render his sudden transformation from a bitter enemy to a humble disciple and friend of Jesus Christ one of the marvels of the ages.

The intellectual and moral character of Paul makes it impossible to believe that he was duped or deceived. Paul was no dreamer or mere speculator in theories of religion. He was a hard-headed and intensely practical man. Any one who will read Paul's writings will be ready to admit that he was a man of robust and powerful mind. The fact was that Paul was suddenly confronted with the great supernatural truth of the Gospel. The risen and glorified Christ revealed himself to this earnest but bitter and bigoted young man, and all his unbelief and hatred of Christ and Christianity went down in a moment, never to appear again. To Paul that hour was the most wonderful and glorious in his history. Years afterward, when he stood before Agrippa and Festus, he recounted confidently and lovingly the events of that day when on the way to Damascus the Lord had first revealed himself to him, and with great joy and pride exclaimed at the conclusion of his defense, "Wherefore, O King Agrippa, I was not disobedient unto the heavenly vision."

The words of Christ to Paul on the Damascus road were not flattering. They recalled a simple scene which Paul had no doubt witnessed many times that very day—an ox, goaded by his driver, kicking back angrily against the sharp prick in the ox-goad which the driver carried, only to wound himself the deeper. There is nothing in the Bible to minister to our egotism or sense of self-sufficiency. We are assured everywhere that our self-righteousness is but filthy rags in the sight of God. We are told that we are never in so pitiable a condition as when in our arrogant pride we consider ourselves rich and having need of nothing. The Lord declares that that is the time when we are poor and blind and naked. We are farthest away from salvation when, dead in trespasses and in sins, we are unconscious of our great and terrible need of divine forgiveness.

To any who are thus asleep in the midst of awful danger, who are congratulating yourselves that you are not so bad as many others, and have not such imperative need of a Savior as some whom you deem more unfortunate sinners, in the words of divine truth I would shout in your ears heaven's alarming rebuke, "Awake thou that sleepest, and arise from the dead, and Christ shall shine upon thee!" Oh, that it might be with you as it was with Paul on that day when heaven's light poured about him, and broke down all his pride and left him a trembling, humble seeker after salvation!

But the great message of all is couched in these words of Jesus, "It is hard for thee to kick against the goad." There is a truth in that statement which I pray God the Holy Spirit may help me to bring so clearly to your minds and hearts that it may be to some of you "a savor of life unto life." The thought that burns in these words for me is, that altho the entrance upon a path of sin is like a wide gate, and tho the way to death is broad, yet at every step God has mercifully placed the pricks of warning and rebuke and punishment to sharply recall the poor sinner to the fact that he is on the wrong path, and to arouse within his soul forebodings of a judgment to come.

We are assured by these words of Jesus that Paul had not been without these merciful prickings of the divine goad. No doubt when he listened to that wonderful address of Stephen—and his keen mind could not help but appreciate the clearness with which Stephen traced the hand of God in the history of mankind from Abraham down to the fulfilment of all the prophecies in the death and resurrection of Jesus Christ—it was hard for his prejudice to stand out against this logical and powerful appeal to his reason. And when he saw the undaunted courage of Stephen, beset by foes upon every hand, and beheld his face shining like an angel, it was hard to believe that there was not something supernatural, something divine, giving support to this heroic young man in his great emergency. And then the great test came. Paul was present when the bitter wrath of the mob could not be restrained longer, and they hurled their cruel stones against the unresisting form of that gentle Christian hero. Paul saw him kneeling down and lifting his bruised and blood-stained face toward the sky. Paul heard first his triumphant shout, "Behold, I see the heavens opened, and the Son of man standing on the right hand of God," and afterward his tender pleading for his enemies, "Lay not this sin to their charge." It must have been hard for Paul to kick against the goad in that hour. There he stood consenting to this young man's death. The men who were murdering him had laid down their outer garments at his feet, and Stephen's tender prayer was for him as much as for them. No doubt his aroused conscience told him that there must be something noble and divine about a religion that could take away from a man's soul, when suffering such cruel provocation, all desire for vengeance, and all anger, and give such peace and victory over the sense of pain and the fear of death.

My unconverted friends, have you not known what it was to kick against the goad like that? Surely you must have known some Christian friends who so lived in the spirit of Christ that you have not been able to doubt their honesty, or the reality of the religion which strengthened and comforted them. Some of you have had devoted Christian parents. There was that noble father whose rugged Christian honesty has been a sort of sheet-anchor which has never permitted you to drift entirely away from your childhood's faith. There was that tender, gentle mother, who taught you to pray "Now I lay me down to sleep"; she who sang Christian lullabies about the gateway of your opening consciousness and followed the wayward steps of your advancing years with her holy benediction. You can not doubt the sincerity and reality of her Christian life. Ah, there has been a goad it has been hard for you to kick against. Again and again the memory of that loving face has called you to strict account. God grant it may not be in vain!

Some of you have been pricked deeply by the departure of friends who have gone away into the skies, leaving a shining pathway behind them that has not only beckoned you to follow, but has made your own path of selfishness and worldliness seem darker and more unsatisfactory than ever. Some of you have had little children of your own whom you loved more than your own lives, and they have sickened and died out of your arms, and beside the little coffin that seemed to hold your own aching heart you have listened with quickened ears and a new intelligence to the words of Jesus: "Suffer the little children to come unto me, and forbid them not: for of such is the kingdom of heaven." And as the minister came to the words, "In heaven their angels do always behold the face of my Father which is in heaven," your heart has cried out after them, and you have said: "I must not miss heaven! I must follow my darlings thither! I must find them again!" Ah, you know, and the tender Christ knows, it has been hard for you to kick against these goads, and go back again into the path of indifference and sin. If you are lost at last, if in the great day of judgment you are shut out in bitter remorse and everlasting loneliness from those loved ones who are inside heaven's gate, it will not be because God has not faithfully warned you, and rebuked you, and pricked you to the very heart, again and again, in seeking to turn your steps from the way of death.

But, alas! it is the tragedy of human life that, hard as it is, you may kick against the goad—tho it hurt you, tho it wound you sore—until you harden your soul against the merciful warnings of God. Do not, I beg you, seek to crush out the conscience that rebukes you for your sin and prompts you to make your peace with God. There may come a day when you would give everything you possess if you could only make that seared conscience as tender again as of yore.

> "'Good-by,' I said to my conscience—
> 'Good-by for aye and aye,'
> And I put her hands off harshly,
> And turned my face away;
> And conscience, smitten sorely,
> Returned not from that day.

"But a time came when my spirit
 Grew weary of its pace;
And I cried: 'Come back, my conscience,
 I long to see thy face.'
But conscience cried: 'I can not;
 Remorse sits in my place.'"

And remorse often comes too late for remedy.

A sad thing happened not long ago in the Alps. A young physician had determined to reach the heights of Mont Blanc. He accomplished the feat, and the little village of Chamouni was illuminated in his honor; the flag was flying from the hut on the mountainside—that told the story of his victory. But after he had ascended, and descended in safety as far as the wayside hut, he wanted to be freed from the rope, and insisted that he could go alone. The guide remonstrated with him, told him it was not safe; but he was tired of the rope, and declared that he would be free of it. The guide had to yield. The young man had gone only a short distance when his foot slipped on the ice, and he could not keep himself from sliding down the inclined icy steeps. The rope was gone, so the guide could not help him or hold him back, and on a shelving piece of ice, far below, he met a cruel and awful death. The bells had rung, the village had been illuminated in honor of his success; but, in spite of it all, in a foolish and wicked moment he refused to be guided; he was tired of the rope.

Are any tired of the rope of God's law and the restraints of his grace? Are you kicking against the goad that would arouse you to your danger, and scorning the hand of the Guide—that living hand that was pierced with nails on the cross, that is outstretched to lead you in paths of righteousness and safety? Do not, I plead with you, make such a fatal decision; but rather follow the example of Paul, who, when he saw how wrong he had been, cried out trembling, "Lord, what wilt thou have me to do?"

The last time Dr. A. J. Gordon, of Boston, was out of his bed until they placed him in his coffin, was when he went, sick and weary, to speak to the young Baptists of Boston, and his dying message to those young people was: "Never say no to God." The great-hearted man went on to illustrate it by a missionary anecdote. He told how, when William Carey, the great pioneer missionary of the century, died, some one preached a sermon concerning him, in which he made the strange remark that Carey was inconstant, that he did not know his own mind. To think, said Dr. Gordon, that any one should say that Carey did not know his own mind; Carey, who was not only the greatest missionary, but one of the greatest scholars, of the century, who translated the Bible into something like twenty-six dialects, and who gave nearly all his wealth to missions. How Carey's friend came to the conclusion that he was inconstant was this: Carey had acknowledged that he had left his business to become a missionary to the heathen because he could not say no; he went to India because he could not say no; he engaged himself in the translation of the Bible because he could not say no; and all his life he had done things because he could not say no. He meant that he could not say no to God. He could say no to the world, the flesh, and the devil; he could say no to his own heart's desires, to his own fleshly allurements; but could not and would not say no to God.

My friends, I bring you this same message, and I plead with you that you too will refuse to say no to the tender invitation of the Savior. Yield your heart to him and, it may be trembling like Paul, and groping in the dark at first as he did, yet humbly and trustingly, say, "Lord, what wilt thou have me to do?"

A WARM HAND-GRASP FOR THE MAN IN THE DARK.

"And Ananias departed, and entered into the house; and laying his hands on him said, Brother Saul, the Lord, even Jesus, who appeared unto thee in the way which thou camest, hath sent me, that thou mayest receive thy sight, and be filled with the Holy Ghost. And straightway there fell from his eyes as it were scales, and he received his sight; and he arose and was baptized; and he took food and was strengthened."—*Acts* ix. 17-19 (Rev. Ver.).

WHAT a transformation is here presented in the person and spirit of Paul! Only three days ago he was the pompous representative of the cruel government in its bitter persecution of the despised Christians. He was engaged in this infamous work not because he was drafted into it, but because his heart was hot with anger against them and he took delight in hunting them to the death. But what a change has come over him! That wonderful vision before which he fell to the ground on the highway at noon, and the pleading voice of Christ making himself known to Paul so clearly and reasoning with him with so much tenderness, have broken his heart and scattered all his unbelief to the winds. To his pleading inquiry, "Lord, what wilt thou have me to do?" there is an immediate response.

Some of you have known for a long time that you were sinners against God, and that you were wickedly rebelling against him, and the duty of repenting of your sins and making confession of Christ has been pressed upon you by the Bible, by the preacher, and by the Holy Spirit acting on your own conscience; but your prayer has been, "Lord, I pray thee have me excused." The way to hell is paved with prayers like that. That prayer never opened the door of mercy to a single soul. So long as that petition is on your lips you will go every day deeper into the gloom. Change about, and take the other tack, and let your trembling lips utter the words of Paul, "Lord, what wilt thou have me to do?" That plea is a sure key with which to open the door of salvation.

The immediate response to that appeal is: "Arise, and go into the city, and it shall be told thee what thou must do. And the men which journeyed with him stood speechless, hearing a voice, but seeing no man. And Saul arose from the earth; and when his eyes were opened, he saw no man: but they led him by the hand, and brought him into Damascus. And he was three days without sight, and neither did eat nor drink."

I am not surprised that Paul had no appetite for food during those days of blindness when he was groping his way out of the darkness and the quagmires of sin in which he had been floundering, and climbing up toward the light and on to the solid rock of righteousness. You would not eat or drink or sleep, if you could only see as clearly as did Paul the awful wrong and wickedness of your sins against God; if you could see as he saw that in your rejection of the Savior you have been stamping contemptuously on the very cross of Jesus and counting the blood of the covenant an unholy thing. Better a thousand times these days of weakness and agony that are to issue in forgiveness and salvation, than to go on in the path of sin with a strong body and a gay heart, filling up the cup of wrath that after a while will have to be drunk in unspeakable sorrow down to the bitter dregs!

But the loving Savior does not keep Paul long in the slough of despond. Living in another part of the city is a saint of God, a man who fears God and keeps his commandments, whose heart is sensitive to the Holy Spirit and in close intimacy and fellowship with Jesus Christ. "To him said the Lord in a vision, Ananias. And he said, Behold, I am here, Lord. And the Lord said unto him, Arise, and go into the street which is called Straight, and inquire in the house of Judas for one called Saul, of Tarsus; for, behold, he prayeth, and hath seen in a vision a man named Ananias coming in, and putting his hand on him, that he might receive his sight. Then Ananias answered, Lord, I have heard by many of this man, how much evil he hath done to thy saints at Jerusalem; and here he hath authority from the chief priests to bind all that call on thy name. But the Lord said unto him, Go thy way; for he is a chosen vessel unto me, to bear my name before the Gentiles, and kings, and the children of Israel; for I will show him how great things he must suffer for my name's sake."

How lifelike is this quibble of Ananias about the dangerous character of Paul. It seems very silly in the mouth of Ananias, to hear him trying to instruct the Lord regarding Paul, as if he was ignorant concerning the very mission on which he was sending his servant. But with great forbearance and tenderness the Lord tells Ananias to go his way and do his duty, and he will take care of the result. I would to God every one of us who are Christians could learn this lesson! It is the old quibble, presented over and over again, concerning every call to duty which seems to the eye of our sense beyond the power of our unaided human ability to perform.

Some monstrous sin, like the liquor traffic, gorging itself on a hundred thousand of the fairest and brightest of our brothers and sisters every year, torturing them by inches, marring and poisoning and rotting their bodies, wrecking their minds, defiling and brutalizing their souls until, maimed, broken-hearted, and despairing, they are cast into a drunkard's hell—all this goes on before our eyes, and tho we loathe it and wish it were stopped, we take up with Ananias's mumbling quibble, "It has the authority of the chief priests," and therefore nothing can be done. Do you not suppose that God, who has said in his Word that "no drunkard shall inherit the kingdom of God," and who gave his Son "to seek and to save the lost," knows all about the power of wickedness? It is for us to go our way in the name of our Master, expecting, not in our own strength, but abetted by the invincible power of God, to see this devil and every devil "fall like lightning from heaven."

We may see also the folly of selecting some persons as beyond the power of Christ's mercy to save and redeem. Ananias could see in Paul only a creature to be feared. He remembered only his bloody deeds and evil reputation, and no doubt thought he would be thrusting his head into a trap if he went to him on an errand of salvation. But Jesus Christ saw in him the man which his divine grace was to make of him. He saw him humbled and purified, with all his great capabilities devoted to righteousness—the mightiest force for Christianity in his generation.

Oh, I wish we could see humanity through Christ's eyes! We pass by our neighbors who have wicked habits that make them disagreeable and unlovable to us, and we scarcely think it worth while to undertake their salvation. But if we could only look underneath all these ugly and sinful habits, and apprehend the good it would be possible for these people to perform, the sweet and holy lives they might live if once won to Christ, with what earnestness and enthusiasm we would work for their salvation!

John Bunyan was a wretched, swearing, drunken tinker. If nobody had thought him worth saving, how much poorer would both earth and heaven be to-day?

Jerry McAuley was a drunken river thief and a jailbird, degraded and defiled by inheritance and by practise; but the man who had the spiritual vision and divine optimism which made him persist in securing the salvation of Jerry McAuley, put more than a thousand priceless jewels in the Savior's crown.

John B. Gough was considered a hopeless drunkard. He was bankrupt in character and in purse. But a humble disciple of Christ saw the jewel underneath all the mud and defilement, and coveted him for the service of the Lord. How blessed the man who led John B. Gough to Christ, for he in turn won tens of thousands to righteousness!

There is nothing too hard for God. We go not to this war at our own charges. We may have on the whole armor of God, and with us constantly the presence of the Holy Spirit that shall make us more powerful than all that can be against us.

Ananias, at last convinced and aroused to do his duty, "went his way and entered into the house." Let me urge upon you the necessity of putting the impressions of the divine Spirit at once into action. Holy meditations, hearts swelling with good desires, sympathy which even moves us to tears, are all wasted, even worse than wasted, if they do not communicate themselves to hand, and feet, and voice, and cause us to arise and "go our way, and enter into the house" where the opportunity to do service for Christ awaits us. We ought to be very watchful for opportunities for service. Of Christians it is said: "They watch for souls as they that must give account."

What great things sometimes turn on little

pivots. One day in the city an accident had happened to a person which a doctor's skill could have instantly relieved; and as the doctor, driving rapidly to the help of the patient, came to the intersection of the streets, he inquired of one standing there which way to take to the sufferer's house. The man pointed in the wrong direction, the doctor was carried far out of his way, and before he could get back the patient was dead. The opportunity could not be recalled; the moment when a life might have been saved by a simple wave of the hand was gone forever. Christian friends, which way are you pointing to these people who are rapidly passing on the way of life and are often inquiring, "Which path shall I take?"

A young man had a pen in his hand with the purpose of signing a pledge, but, on being told that the Christian lady who was urging him to take the path of safety herself drank wine, he dropped his pen, and said, "If she drinks, I may." He went on his way of temptation unfortified, and staggered into a drunkard's grave. She had lost her great opportunity.

When Ananias reached the house where Paul was, he entered upon his mission with rare skill and wisdom. One can not imagine a more beautiful method of leading a soul into the light than that taken by Ananias. Putting his hands on him he said, "Brother Saul, the Lord, even Jesus, that appeared unto thee in the way as thou camest, hath sent me, that thou mightest receive thy sight, and be filled with the Holy Ghost." The brotherly spirit and tenderness of sympathy expressed in his action and in his words must have been infinitely soothing and comforting to Paul's wounded heart. Christian work can not be done successfully in any other spirit than that. That same spirit of brotherly fellowship and loving solicitude must possess our hearts and clothe us with a divine gentleness that will make us winning messengers for the Savior.

In one of the battles of the war of the rebellion, a gunner fell across his gun with a mortal wound in his head, and over his lifeless body bent in despairing grief a forlorn, powder-smoked boy of fifteen. He had just kissed the lifeless face, and stood with quivering lips and heart-breaking grief gazing into the dear face that was stiffening in the grasp of death. The chaplain, just then coming up, heard the poor boy say: "He is dead, and I'm all alone now in the world." The last of his brothers had fallen, his father and mother were dead, and he was without friends or home. "No, you are not alone," said the chaplain, as he tenderly put his arms around the heart-broken boy. That unloosed the fountain of his grief, and the first tears began to flow down over his powder-stained cheeks. The Christian sympathy expressed in the good man's words and actions mellowed his aching heart and the thought of a new-found friend gave him relief. That brotherly act won that boy to Christ, and he lived to be a noble Christian man who has given in his turn the same brotherly embrace to many another disheartened soul.

If we are to be soul-winners we must have the winning spirit—the love which forbears and forgives, and suffers long and is kind; the love which helps us to put ourselves in our brother's place and causes us to bring our message of good news with the spirit of gentle fellowship that will not give offense. We are not to drive men into the kingdom of God, but to win them; and many times a spirit of brotherly kindness exhibited by us in temporal matters makes it possible for us to win in the higher realm of the soul.

I remember the story of another chaplain in the army during the same war, who was passing over the field when he saw lying upon the ground a soldier who had been wounded.

He happened to have his Bible under his arm, and he stooped down and said to the man: "Would you like me to read you something that is in the Bible?"

The wounded man said: "I am so thirsty, I would rather have a drink of water."

The chaplain hurried off, as quickly as possible, and brought the water.

After the man had drunk the water he said: "Could you lift my head, and put something under it?"

The chaplain took off his own overcoat, rolled it up, and, tenderly lifting him, put it as a pillow for his tired head to rest on.

"Now," said the man, "if I only had something over me; I am so cold."

There was only one thing the chaplain could do, and that was to take his coat off and cover the man. As he did so, the wounded soldier looked up in his face and said:

"For God's sake, if there is anything in that book that makes a man do for another what you have done for me, let me hear it."

There is infinite meaning in that story. The world could not know God until it saw him in the face of Jesus Christ. And multitudes in our day are so carried away by worldliness, are so oppressed by the burdens or seduced by the pleasures and gayeties of life, that they will never see Jesus unless they see him in our lives. If they are to be won to the Lord, the divine brotherhood of Jesus must be in us and be thus used by the Holy Spirit for their salvation.

As Ananias talked with Paul in this brotherly spirit, the scales fell from his eyes, and he entered into the light. The joy and power of the Holy Ghost came upon him. And on the first opportunity he proclaimed his new-found faith that Jesus was the Son of God.

To you who are not Christians, I want to lay emphasis on Paul's discovery of the divinity of Jesus. It is not a mere man whom we preach unto you. He took upon himself our flesh and was born under the law that he might redeem those that were under the law, and as the captain of our salvation he was made perfect through sufferings, being tempted in all points like as we are. But he was not a victim; he was a heavenly Prince who put aside the glory of heaven that he might of his own accord bear our sins on the cross. He who met Saul the persecutor, on the way to Damascus, and, convincing his judgment and softening his heart, transformed him into Paul the Christian, is able to forgive your sins, to break the bondage of your iniquity, and lift you into the sweet atmosphere of a holy life.

You have heard many sermons like this, portraying the Scripture truth in these Bible stories, and have gone away as tho it were only a picture for your entertainment, and your life has gone on as before. God grant it may be different now! This Word of God may be infinitely more than a picture to you if you will open your heart to receive it.

An old woman was living in Scotland in the most abject poverty. It was understood in the community that she had a son in America who was prosperous, and her neighbors wondered that he would permit his mother to endure such suffering. One day one of them ventured to ask about the matter.

"Does your son never send you any money?"

"No," reluctantly answered the mother; yet, eager to defend her absent boy, she said, "but he writes me nice long letters and sends me a pretty picture in almost every one of them."

"Where are these pictures?" asked the neighbor. "May I see them?"

"Why, certainly," answered the old lady. She hobbled to a shelf and took down the old Bible, and there between the leaves lay the "pictures" that her son had been sending her from America through all the years.

What were they? Nothing more nor less than bank-notes, each for a considerable amount. During all her time of need and poverty she had had lying there in abundance riches to satisfy all her wants. But in her ignorance she had only looked at the pictures and kept them because they were the reminders of her far-off son.

Some of you have been treating the Bible that way. You have read or you have heard the minister read these stories of redeeming love, and you have thought them pretty pictures, but have gone on with starving, sinful hearts as tho there was nothing else in them for you. O brother, sister, they are more than pictures—they are bank-notes, they are drafts on the mercy of heaven, and riches inexhaustible are in them for your soul! What Christ did for Paul he is ready to do for you. May this be the hour when your poverty shall pass away and your soul be made rich indeed!

A MAN WHO FAILED ONCE, BUT WON ON A SECOND CHANCE.

"And Barnabas and Saul returned from Jerusalem, when they had fulfilled their ministration, taking with them John whose surname was Mark."—*Acts* xii. 25 (Rev. Ver.).

"Now Paul and his company set sail from Paphos, and came to Perga in Pamphylia: and John departed from them and returned to Jerusalem."—*Acts* xiii. 13 (Rev. Ver.).

"And after some days Paul said unto Barnabas, Let us return now and visit the brethren in every city wherein we proclaimed the word of the Lord, and see how they fare. And Barnabas was minded to take with them John also, who was called Mark. But Paul thought not good to take with them him who withdrew from them from Pamphylia, and went not with them to the work. And there arose a sharp contention, so that they parted asunder one from the other, and Barnabas took Mark with him, and sailed away unto Cyprus; but Paul chose Silas, and went forth, being commended by the brethren to the grace of the Lord."—*Acts* xv. 36–40 (Rev. Ver.).

"Take Mark, and bring him with thee: for he is useful to me."—2 *Tim.* iv. 11 (Rev. Ver.).

THESE brief Scriptures do not make a very long biography, but when we pause to read between the lines they tell a wonderfully interesting and suggestive story concerning the experiences of John Mark. This young man was one of the earliest Christians. His mother's house was a hotel on the underground railroad of early Christianity. In the old slavery days in this country there used to be what was known as "the underground railroad," along which slaves escaping from the South made their way with great secrecy and many fears toward Canada and freedom. On these routes were certain farmhouses owned by great-hearted men and women who were willing to run the risk of loss by making their homes houses of welcome for these poor wretches who were flying from slavery to liberty. The house of Mary, the mother of Mark, was such a home for the early Christians. There they were always sure of welcome and such comfort as her house afforded. It was in this house that the Christians gathered to pray for Peter on that terrible night when he had been sentenced by Herod to die on the morrow. All through the hours of the night they prayed until Peter, having been rescued by the angel, sought out the house of Mary and knocked at the gate. When the little damsel Rhoda came down to open it and saw that it was Peter, her heart was so glad that she forgot even to open the gate, but ran back shouting at the top of her voice that their prayers were answered and Peter himself stood at the gate. Poor souls!

they could not believe it at first; it seemed too good to be true, and they feared he was already dead and that this was his ghost. But it was Peter, sure enough, and that prayer-meeting broke up in great joy.

It was a precious privilege to be brought up in a home like that, where the greatest men and women among the early Christians were coming and going. To breathe such an atmosphere in one's youth is a glorious boon, and one who has had such an opportunity can never thank God enough for it. How many there are who owe a priceless debt of thanksgiving on account of the Christian homes in which they were born and reared.

It seems very natural that John Mark, brought up in such a home, listening to the conversations of such men as Peter and Barnabas and Paul and Silas, should desire to give his own life to the ministry of Christ and become a bearer of this good news of salvation to those in distant lands. And so when Barnabas and Paul were about to set out on a great preaching tour he gladly joined them and entered hopefully on his career as a messenger of Jesus Christ. No doubt his mother Mary was both rejoiced and saddened to see him go—rejoiced that her son was to go forth in such noble company to be a witness for the Master, and saddened that she was left behind and should miss his dear presence in her daily life. O young man! think tenderly and deal generously concerning the mother who has remained at home watching and waiting while you with exulting heart have gone out on your life career. You have had your lonely and homesick hours, too, but the heaviest burden is carried by the hearts that stay at home. When tempted to forsake the path of righteousness and walk in the way of sin, remember again that anxious, loving heart who sent you out with her prayer and benediction, and resolve to die sooner than say or do that which would bring a blush of shame to her pure face.

Surely, any one prophesying of the future would have said that no one could have a better chance of winning an honorable and glorious place among the early Christian heroes than John Mark. But the prospect was soon sadly darkened. Only a brief period had passed, and they had just got well under way on their journey, when Mark abruptly terminated his association with his friends and teachers and returned home, greatly to the sorrow of Paul and Barnabas. We do not know why he took this course, but we know that his reasons were not satisfactory to Paul, and his conduct was such that this great missionary lost all faith in him and refused to have him in his company five years later when he had changed his mind and wished for the second time to enter on his vocation as a worker for Christ.

It was doubtless a combination of reasons working together which brought about the desertion of Mark and caused him to make shipwreck of the greatest opportunity of his life. He was very young, and was perhaps at first attracted by the novelty of the journey and the strange habits and customs of the people they met; but this soon wore away and the hardship and danger remained. It could not have been for the lack of interesting experiences, for during the short term of his service he had witnessed the awful judgment on Elymas the sorcerer, and the glorious conversion of Sergius Paulus. Yet in spite of these manifestations of the presence of God with them, and the mighty possibilities within the reach of their ministry, Mark threw it all up and went home. What motive can have turned him back? Matthew Henry says, "Either he did not like the work, or he wanted to go see his mother." Quaint old John Trapp says that Mark left them because they were then to take a tedious and dangerous journey over the high mountains of Taurus, and, his ardor having evaporated a little, he sought his own ease by returning home.

Whatever was the cause, we may be sure that John Mark repented it many a long day thereafter.

A mother like his would rather have heard of his death in honorable service than to have seen his face as a coward and a deserter. It was five years before he saw Paul and Barnabas again. Think how much he lost in missing that opportunity for association with Paul through his most vigorous and fruitful years. There never was a college or theological school on the earth that would have been equal to the training, the inspiration, the soul-culture of five years of shoulder-to-shoulder, heart-to-heart fellowship with Paul in those glowing, blazing days of his missionary conquest!

Not only did he lose all this, but when the five years were passed, and God in his infinite mercy had roused him from his lethargy and defeat, and encouraged him to try again, he suffered the shame and humiliation of being refused association and fellowship by the greatest man of his age. And so that one foolish and wicked act, that one cowardly backsliding and desertion, cost him all possibility of associating with Paul throughout the years of his greatest power as a minister. It was not until the great preacher was an old man that Mark was to know again his sympathy and love.

I pray that the Holy Spirit may impress this lesson very deeply on the hearts that need it! We can never in cowardice desert our post and refuse to do our duty without submitting ourselves to fearful loss and heavy penalty. Some of you have been reading your own autobiography in the story of John Mark. You, too, were called in your youth into the church of Jesus Christ. You rejoiced in the glad consciousness that your sins were forgiven and that you were chosen to bear witness for the Savior. Like young Mark you rejoiced in the associations of the church. You delighted in the talk of those who had long known Christ and whose ardent testimony roused your ambition to do valiant service for the Lord. You looked ahead for ten or twenty years or more and pictured yourself as a middle-aged man or woman, devoted to Christ, and as pure and holy in your fidelity to the service of the church as were those noble saints who had won your admiration and your confidence. Alas, that any shadow should ever have come over a life that had so bright a morning of Christian hopefulness and promise! But there came a time when you stood before your mountains and trembled for fear. The day came when you were called upon to endure hardness for the Master's sake, and your treacherous heart, like the foolish Israelites in the wilderness, longed for the leeks and onions and flesh-pots of Egypt, even with its bondage. And so you fell away. Not all at once, perhaps; but step by step, little by little, you were drawn back into the world, until now it may be that your heart is harder and you are farther away from God than before you first pledged him your service.

Now if I am speaking to any such backslidden soul, I know if you are honest with yourself you will bear me witness that the saddest mistake of your life was when you deserted Jesus Christ. In your best hours, when you are your highest and noblest self, you would give anything within your power to buy back your peace with God, your joyous fellowship with Jesus Christ; to regain the hope of usefulness and the promise of spiritual conquest and heavenly triumph the vision of which once animated your soul and made glorious your daily life.

Let no man think it is a light thing to fall away from God's fellowship and love. Alas! many who do so never return. Many a young man has fallen away like John Mark, but, like Samson, who was also reared in a godly home, whose young manhood was animated with noble ambitions and whose early career was glorified with the presence of God, has fallen away to come back no more, and has died, in blindness and bondage and shame, the death of a suicide.

This sad truth was illustrated recently in a Western city. The poor victim was one of the most successful merchants in that great city; he associated with men of prominence, was a member of the leading clubs, and had an open door to all that society has to give. He lived in a splendid mansion on the favorite street of millionaires and merchant princes, and around him were his family and admiring friends. But neither his beautiful home nor his business prosperity could satisfy a heart that had wrenched itself away from God. All the treasures he had gathered became as ashes in his grasp. Who can tell the torture and agony that must have driven his soul when on one of the most beautiful days of autumn he turned his back upon all that for which he had labored, went down to the lake over whose blue waters he had often looked with delight, and, as the light was dawning, by one mad plunge in the cold waters sought to end in their dark depths a life which he could no longer bear. Ah, it is an awful thing, having once tasted of the good word of life, to desert one's post and go back into worldliness and sin!

But in the story of Mark there is a message of hope. Five years had passed away after his desertion, and Paul and Barnabas had returned from their journeyings in great joy and triumph. After a while they decided to go again and visit the churches which they had formed in their long missionary tour, and build them up in the faith. John Mark had now come to his senses and earnestly desired that he might accompany these great preachers again. But Paul, remembering his former desertion, would not consent to have him of the party. Barnabas, however, who was Mark's cousin, believed in the young man and plead that he should be given another trial. Paul refusing to permit this, they separated, and Paul, choosing Silas as his companion, departed in one direction, while Barnabas took Mark and went in another. The result shows that Barnabas was right and Paul was wrong. We have every reason to believe that Mark fully appreciated the second opportunity and was ever afterward a most faithful and efficient witness for Christ. One of the surest evidences of this is that Paul in his old age, in his letter to Timothy, asks him to bring Mark with him to be his associate, and declares concerning him, "He is useful to me." What a victory that was for Mark! It must have been a proud day for him when Timothy showed him Paul's letter and assured him that the great veteran missionary, who had once been so disgusted with him, now believed in him thoroughly and desired to have him as a fellow worker in the Gospel.

Let any of you to whom this message comes with special personal application take it with comfort to your hearts and seize at once the new chance which God is now offering to you in Jesus

Christ. We can not bring back the past. You have made loss and must abide by it unto eternity; but, thank God! there is a new chance, and there is hope and salvation in it, if you will accept it. Because you have failed once is no reason why, with added wisdom and experience and the failure of the past to warn you, you shall not now enter upon a Christian experience that shall be crowned with glorious victory. Come back to Christ now! To-day is the day of salvation. If ye will hear his voice, harden not your hearts.

Do not dally with this opportunity, for another like it may never come. A convict in prison, under sentence of death, was very anxious to get access to the governor that he might plead with him for a pardon. One day a gentleman of unpretending appearance visited his cell and spoke to him very kindly, but without producing any special impression upon him.

After the gentleman had gone some one said to the prisoner, "Did you know that that was the governor?"

"Oh," he said, "why didn't I know it, that I might have asked him to pardon me?"

Opportunities of salvation thus come unheralded and unrecognized and pass away forever. Oh that I had the ability to arrest your attention, arouse your conscience, and summon your will, so that every power of your nature might be concentrated on the offer of salvation which Jesus your Savior makes you now.

Do not wait to make yourself any better. Do not try in your own strength to get back some of the ground you have lost. Christ came to save sinners, and if you will come just as you are, a poor sinner, crying out, with the publican mentioned in the Gospel record, "God be merciful to me a sinner!" you may be sure of a loving welcome.

There is a story of a great monarch who was accustomed on certain set occasions to entertain all the beggars of the city. Around him were placed his courtiers, all clothed in rich apparel; the beggars sat at the same table in their rags of poverty. Now it came to pass that on a certain day one of the courtiers had spoiled his silken apparel, so that he dared not put it on, and he felt, "I can not go to the king's feast to-day, for my robe is foul." He sat weeping till the thought struck him: "To-morrow, when the king holds his feast, some will come as courtiers happily decked in their beautiful array, but others will come and be made quite as welcome who will be dressed in rags. Well, well," said he, "so long as I may see the king's face and sit at the royal table, I will enter among the beggars." So he put on the rags of a beggar and was welcomed to the king's table.

My friend, this is just your case. You have spoiled the silken robe of your purity, you can only come as a poor sinner. But as such he will welcome you and you shall sit at his table, tho not in rags, for he will clothe you anew in his own righteousness. Only yield your heart to the Gospel message and you shall be able to sing with the poet-saint:

> "Jesus, thy blood and righteousness
> My beauty are, my glorious dress;
> 'Midst flaming worlds, in these arrayed,
> With joy shall I lift up my head."

THE CURE OF SOULS.

"He had faith to be made whole."—*Acts* xiv. 9 (Rev. Ver.).

PAUL and Barnabas had come to Lystra in their great missionary preaching tour. Luke with almost epigrammatic brevity describes their conduct there by saying, "And there they preached the gospel." We do not know whether they preached in a hall, or a temple, or in the street; but it was most probably in the open air. We do not know a great deal about the audience, except that there was a good crowd, and among them there was a priest of Jupiter, and a poor cripple who had been such all his life and had never been able to walk with his weak, crooked legs. Perhaps some one had carried him to the place where Paul was talking, to gratify his curiosity or to bring a little touch of freshness and newness into his dull life. It is hard to be a cripple and to be unable to help oneself, to see others walk and run carelessly as tho it were nothing at all, while we are chained to the bed or chair and must depend on somebody's kindness to carry us about. It is hard to be a cripple now under the most favorable circumstances. Many a rich man with rheumatic limbs would give half his fortune and more if he could walk and run equal to the newsboy who sells him his morning paper. But to have been a cripple in those old days, when easy-chairs and rolling-chairs were unknown, and hospitals and modern surgery and medicine had never been dreamed of, must have been pitiful indeed.

Of all the people in the congregation, this cripple attracted Paul's attention most. The heart of Paul was thoroughly permeated with the spirit of the Christ whom he preached. Whoever had the greatest need of the Gospel message made the greatest demand on Paul's attention and self-denying service. Jesus Christ came to die for a race of lost sinners not because they were good, but because they were bad; not because they had any worth or merit, but because they were unlovable and lost and without hope. So Paul felt that the man who was in the worst plight and whom nobody else cared for was the special prize which it was above all else his duty to capture for his Master.

All we know about the sermon is that Luke declares it was the Gospel. But judging from the other sermons of Paul which we have read, we know very well some of the things that were in it.

Paul told that wondering crowd of idol-worshipers of "the living God" who is over all, from whose hand comes every good and perfect gift; who created man in his own image and likeness, and watched after him with tender compassion and love as he went astray into paths of sin and brought upon himself sorrow and remorse and ruin. Then he told of the love of God that sought out a way of salvation for poor lost sinners, and assured them, no doubt, as he afterward did in his letter to the Romans, that, tho "the wages of sin is death," the great gift of God is eternal life through Jesus Christ our Lord. Then he told of the coming of Jesus, of his pure life, of his deeds of mercy and healing. How he opened the eyes of the blind; how he made deaf men hear and dumb men speak; how he even cleansed lepers and brought back the dead to life; and that finally, when he had been slain upon the cruel cross, and his dead body put away in a stone tomb with a sealed door and guarded with soldiers, he had burst asunder the bands of death, and risen from the dead, and is alive forevermore, the friend and Savior of sinners.

Then Paul with glowing face and moist eyes told the wonderful story of his own meeting with Jesus Christ. We are sure he did that, for he never failed, no matter what the character of the audience—whether he were preaching in the street or making defense before kings—to seize upon every opportunity to bear that witness to his Lord. And so we are sure he told over again, that day in Lystra, of his early hatred of Christ, and of his persecution of the Christians, and how he went up to Damascus with authority to put them in prison or even persecute them to the death; and how as he went in the way he met the Lord. He told of the light that shone round about them, and of the pleading words of Christ, "Why persecutest thou me? It is hard for thee to kick against the goad!" that had broken his heart and melted his hatred into love; and that from that day, having obtained the help of God, he had been faithful unto the heavenly vision.

Now just imagine how all this sounded in the ears of that crippled man lying there on the ground before Paul. You have heard it all so often that there is danger of its losing its power to interest and awaken and save you. God forbid that such should be the case! But this poor fellow was hearing it for the first time. He was hearing it, too, out of a deep consciousness of his great need.

It may be that he was not greatly interested in the opening of Paul's argument. Perhaps he said to himself: "The knowledge of the gods and of such wonderful people as this Jewish Messiah is of no great interest to a poor cripple like me. It may be all right for scholars, and travelers who can go about the world, to store up interesting knowledge like that; but what chance is there for a poor crooked-legged fellow like me to know anything?"

But when Paul got to the place where he began to tell about the ministry of Jesus, and how he went about doing good, and of the different people he healed, and that many of them were poor and had nothing to pay—ah! I can see the flash of interest in his eyes and the aroused and alert attitude of his head as he watches Paul. Underneath his interest a reverie is running in his mind. He is saying to himself: "Why! the man who could open the eyes of one who was born blind could straighten the limbs of one who was born a cripple." And then when Paul came to the story of the bringing of Lazarus from the grave, he could hardly keep from shouting aloud: "That man could heal me! If he can bring a dead man back to life, then if he ever comes this way I am just as good as healed!"

Then he settles himself to listen, trying to learn where this great Healer is now. Perhaps this strange preacher is only his forerunner, and the Master himself will soon be along. And then Paul tells of the arrest of Jesus, of the trial before Pilate, of the crown of thorns, and of the cross on Golgotha. Oh, the wonder and sorrow that crept into that poor cripple's face! His heart sank, and the new, strange hope that had made life seem worth living again died down in his soul. His poor, pallid face bore witness to the heartache within, and he groaned as Paul came to the place in the story where they put the dead body of Jesus away in Joseph's tomb.

But something in Paul's attitude, and some overpowering hopefulness in his tone and the flash of his eye, aroused him to listen to the wonderful story of the resurrection. Yet it all seemed vague and unreal until Paul began to tell his own personal experience. Oh! the power of personal experience. Not one of you, whatever your eloquence or your learning, will ever preach any gospel equal in attractive and saving power to that which you proclaim when, with humility and simplicity, you speak of the loving-kindness of Jesus Christ in the forgiveness of your own sins, in the salvation of your own soul.

And so the poor fellow followed Paul all the way from Jerusalem to Damascus, and listened with throbbing heart and renewing hope to the story of Paul's conversion. The deep significance of the change wrought in Paul impressed him, and made him feel that after all that was a greater miracle than the healing of crippled limbs.

Now Paul had been watching all this undercurrent of tragedy that was stirring this man's soul; for the record says that Paul had been looking at this man with great interest and attention. There was nothing very uncommon and unusual about that; most public speakers are conscious of delivering their discourse to here and there a face that attracts and holds them with special interest. This is especially true if it be a congregation of strangers and all the faces are new to the speaker. Some one face, it may be, will seize the speaker's attention and hold his gaze and control a certain indefinable undercurrent of his thought throughout his address. Paul was a man of keen spiritual insight, and he had watched the face of this poor cripple and saw as he concluded the story of his own salvation that this man had come to be a believer in Jesus Christ for himself. He saw in the man's eyes his willingness to take Jesus as his Savior, and Paul, "steadfastly beholding him, and perceiving that he had faith to be made whole, said with a loud voice, Stand upright on thy feet. And he leaped and walked."

I want to call special attention to the emphasis laid on the kind of faith which Paul discerned in this man. "He had faith to be made whole." The first element in that faith was that he believed Jesus Christ, who had performed all those wonderful deeds that Paul had recounted, was able and willing to heal him.

Brother, let us apply this to yourself. Is it not true that you have that much faith? Altho there have been times, perhaps, when the devil has tried to make you believe that Christ was only a man like other men, and has no superhuman power to save, yet in your better hours you know that this is not true. You are sure that no mere Galilean youth could have gone out from his carpenter's shop in Nazareth to have launched upon the world the mighty river of saving influence that has filled the earth with churches and schools and hospitals and orphan asylums, and transformed the face of nations, and two thousand years after his death be ever increasing in power over the hearts and lives of men. Your reason and your heart bow down before all this, and in the inner court of your soul you say, "He is the Christ. He is the divine Savior of the world."

You also believe that he is able to save you. There are times, possibly, when the chain of evil habit is specially noticeable to you and seems to hold you like a prisoner in its iron grip, that you have been tempted to feel that there was for you no hope of freedom from this bondage of iniquity. But when you come to consider how great have been the conversions he has wrought, when you think of the ransomed and transformed lives the record of which not only fills the pages of the Bible, but whose testimonies are in every town and city and whose stories are in every prayer-meeting, you do believe that he is able to save you.

Why, then, are you not saved?

It may be that with some the sense of need is not great enough. If that is keeping you back, I pray God that he will uncover to you the depravity of your own heart and show you the terrible danger and peril of this heart-wandering. Sin in the sight of God is an awful thing. It was sin that drove Adam and Eve from the Garden of Eden. It was sin that flooded the world with desolation and disaster. It was sin that rained devastation on Sodom and the cities of the plain. It was sin that pressed down the crown of piercing thorns on the innocent brow of Jesus. It was sin that gave force to every cut of the lash that drew the blood from his bruised and wounded back. It was sin that drove the nails through his hands and feet and pierced him to the heart. It is sin to-day that fills the jails and the prisons. It is sin that is causing strife and quarreling and bitterness and heartache in the homes of the people. It is sin that is driving men and women in the bloom of their years to crime and suicide. Ah, has not sin done aught for you? Has it caused you no tears? Has it caused you no sleepless hours? Has it blighted no flowers of hope in your soul? I do not know what your sin is, but God knows, and you know, and I am certain that if the Holy Spirit will uncover your heart to you now, you will be sure of your need of a Savior—as sure as was that poor cripple at Lystra that he needed the great Healer to cure him.

But if you feel your need, and you believe that Christ is able and willing to save you, why are you not saved? The one element that you lack, which Paul discovered in the poor cripple, is a willingness to act here and now on your faith. Paul as he looked into the eyes of the crippled man saw in him the faith to be healed then and there; and so, looking him straight in the eye that he might understand who was meant, Paul said with a loud voice: "Stand upright on thy feet." And the man responded at once. He never had stood on his feet. But he made no excuses. In this new faith in Christ he made the attempt, and strange sensations ran through his limbs, his veins were on fire with new life, his muscles relaxed, his crooked bones straightened, and he not only stood, but his glad heart expressed its rapture in joyous leaps.

It is that element of faith which you lack, and the power to have that is in yourself.

God has done everything he can for your salvation. Jesus Christ has borne your sins in his own body on the cross. He has tasted death for you. And now the invitation comes to you to act. That is all that is necessary for your healing. You have heard the Gospel and you believe it. What is there for you to do now but obey the commandments of Jesus by confessing him before men and henceforth keeping his words? "Whosoever will may come!" If you will, you may. It took only a moment to save this poor cripple, and it will take but a moment to save you if you determine now to be saved.

Mr. S. Donaldson, the evangelist, tells this interesting story of a soul's salvation: A sailor had been ashore on leave of absence and returned at night partially intoxicated. The ship was connected with the wharf by only a narrow plank about a foot wide, and when he attempted to walk over it, he slipped and fell, but succeeded in seizing hold of the plank. The fright sobered him, and he felt the plank move; but after a quiver or two it stood fast and he hung suspended over the water. He was afraid to move, lest he should bring both plank and himself down into the water. He shouted for help, but there came no reply. Then there came to his mind the text of a sermon he had heard in the Seaman's Bethel: "After death the judgment." He was sure that for him judgment was only another name for condemnation. The beads of perspiration were breaking out on his forehead from fear of death and what would follow. In that awful moment, direct from heaven there flashed before him a vision of Christ the Savior, and in his heart he accepted him. Immediately there came the message that brought peace to the stricken heart. He knew that God had saved him —that he had passed from death unto life. All his anguish and fear of death passed away. But God had work for him to do on this earth. Lights began to move on the wharf, and he was discovered and rescued. Yet he blesses that night, when God by his providence brought him to see his need of a Savior; and tho it is now years ago, he has ever since rejoiced in the Lord, and striven to make known to others the good news that Jesus loves and saves.

This may be your hour of salvation. The cripple at Lystra had been a cripple all his life, but he was healed in a single moment. Sin has hurt and marred you and saddened your life, it may be for many years, but if you will accept the invitation of salvation, your sins may be forgiven and you ransomed from guilt in a single moment. Oh, that the mighty spirit that was in Paul may rest upon me and give me power to look into your eyes and say, "Stand upright on thy feet?" and give you power to respond unto the confession of Christ, and to the salvation of your soul!

A CRY FOR HELP FROM SILENT LIPS.

"A vision appeared to Paul in the night; there was a man of Macedonia standing, beseeching him, and saying, Come over into Macedonia and help us. And when he had seen the vision, straightway we sought to go forth into Macedonia, concluding that God had called us for to preach the gospel unto them."—*Acts* xvi. 9, 10 (Rev. Ver.).

PERHAPS no incident in Paul's life so vividly sets forth the spiritual insight of the man as this. No human messenger had come to them from Macedonia. Macedonia knew nothing about Christ and cared nothing. They were busy with their gains and their gods and knew not the terrible need of their souls that some one should come to them from the living God, and show them how to worship him. But Paul, to whom had come this glorious knowledge of Jesus Christ, saw in their very blindness and ignorance a tremendous appeal for help. His man of Macedonia was the genius of all that heathen world—a typical soul, beating itself against the bars of its own ignorance and sin, and it appealed to Paul with even more pathos than would entreaties from the lips of a man who knew and understood his need.

It is that spiritual insight which we as Christians need. We need to come into such close fellowship with Jesus Christ that, like Paul, we shall see, as Christ sees them, the men and women whom we meet daily, and shall be able to look below the surface of their giddy, self-sufficient lives and behold and pity the hungry heartache which only God can satisfy.

One day a little crippled boy was seated in the corner of a Broadway car in New York City. He was a frail little fellow, and was evidently an intense sufferer from spinal disease. His head and the upper part of his body were enclosed in a network of steel and leather, and an iron brace was tightly strapped to the side of one of his legs. Poverty, too, seemed to be his misfortune. His clothing was of cheap material. There was a hole in every finger of the black cotton gloves worn by his fifteen-year-old sister who accompanied him, and her dress was patched in several places. Tho both were neat and clean, real poverty marked them for its own.

At Thirty-third Street a handsomely dressed young woman boarded the car, and dropped into a seat directly opposite the pair. Tucked in the folds of her coat was a big bunch of fresh double violets, tied with a long purple ribbon, and their fragrant odor at once pervaded the car. The little boy caught the scent, and at once his great brown eyes sought the flowers. Then he whispered something to his sister, who blushed and told him to wait a while. Turning his attention again to the violets, the lad gazed upon them until his eyes grew bright and round, and every few moments he would draw an extra long breath, as if to take in all of the sweet perfume he could. Soon every one in the forward part of the car was watching him. From the look of admiration there grew in those brown eyes an expression of soul-hunger and longing so earnest and deep that it made every heart thrill with sympathy.

The young woman, with changing emotions, glanced uneasily at the boy at intervals, but soon the power of those eyes and the soul they revealed overcame her. With a quick tug she drew the violets from her coat, and with tears springing to her eyes handed them to the boy, purple ribbon and all. Before the child could recover from his great joy she sought the platform and was gone.

There was not a dry eye in all the crowded car. Men and women looked at each other through their tears, so deeply had the little incident, revealing so much of the human heart, moved them.

There ought to be a message in the story for us.

We come into daily association with men and women and children who are heart-hungry for the holiest things, tho they often do not know what it is for which they hunger. But if we live close to God, and breathe the atmosphere of the Christ-spirit, we shall have keen eyes to detect their needs, and sympathetic hearts to bring to their lives the fragrance of heaven.

We always have within our reach the mighty lever of prayer, by which we may move the arm of God in behalf of those who need a revelation of a Savior to their own heart.

Elizabeth Stuart Phelps tells a most beautiful story of Harriet Beecher Stowe. During the latter part of her life, Mrs. Stowe was one of those devout Christian believers whose consecration takes high forms. She had the most implicit faith in prayer, and gave herself to that kind of personal dedication to God which exercises and cultivates it. There came a time when one who was very dear to her seemed about to sink away from the faith in which she trusted, and to which life and sorrow had taught her to cling as only those can who have suffered and found beneath them the warm grip of the Everlasting Arms.

This prospect was a crushing grief to her, and she set herself resolutely to avert the calamity if and while she could. Letter after letter—some of them thirty pages long—found their way from her pen to the foreign town in which German rationalism was doing its worst for the soul she loved. She set the full force of her intellect intelligently to work upon this conflict. She read, she reasoned, she wrote, she argued, she pleaded. Months passed in a struggle whose usefulness seemed a pitiable hope, to be frustrated in the effort.

Then she laid aside her strong pen, and turned to her great faith. As the season of the sacred holiday approached, she shut herself into her room, secluding herself from all but God, and prayed as only such a believer, only such a woman, may. As she had set the full force of her intellect, so now she set the full power of her faith, to work upon her soul's desire. Such prayers never fail of their great end. A few weeks later a letter reached her from over the sea, saying only: "At Christmas-time a light came to me. I see things differently now. I see my way to accept the faith of my fathers; and the belief in Christianity which is everything to you has become reasonable and possible to me at last."

May God help us every one to struggle daily at the throne of grace in behalf of the blind souls who need so much to be able to behold Christ as the One altogether lovely!

Do not many of you now realize that you have been blind to the great interests of your soul? You have lived in a world full of Christ, and yet you have never looked upon him with that heart-look that means salvation. While others were drawing from him the dearest comfort of their souls, you have gone on with the heartache, when you might have reached out your hand and touched the Savior who could have given you peace.

A little girl, the child of a well-known painter, had lost her sight in infancy, and her blindness was supposed to be incurable. A famous oculist in Paris, however, performed a successful operation on her eyes.

Her mother had long been dead, and her father had been her only intimate friend and companion. When she was told that her blindness could be cured, her one thought was that she could see him; and when the cure was complete, and the bandages were removed, she ran to him and, trembling, pored over his features, shutting her eyes now and then, and passing her fingers over his face, as if to make sure that it was he.

The father had a noble head and presence, and his every look and motion were watched by his daughter with the keenest delight. For the first time his constant tenderness and care seemed real to her. If he caressed her, or even looked upon her kindly, it brought the tears to her eyes. "To think," she cried, holding his hand close in hers, "that I had this father so many years and never knew him!"

So I have known people who were born in Christian homes, whose mothers sang them to sleep with songs about Jesus; who grew up in the Sunday-school and knew by heart the story of Christmas, and Calvary, and Easter; who in a dim, blind way had often thought about Christ as the Savior of the world, and the One to whom some time they hoped to come as their personal Redeemer; and yet all his love and sacrifice was vague and unreal and had no vital power over their lives until there came a time when conscience aroused, when the Holy Spirit uncovered to them the sinfulness of their hearts, when as never before they saw the peril of their souls and looked down into the deeper depths toward which sin was leading them; and in the agony of that awakening they turned their tearful eyes toward Christ as their only hope of escape; and Christ, tho long slighted, in the infinite tenderness of his love pardoned their sins, and wiped away their tears, and rejoiced their hearts, and of that new-found Christ they said, like this little girl: "To think that I should have had this Savior all these years and never have come to know him before!"

Do not let anything keep you away from the Christ who offers to save you now. Sometimes the devil holds a man's past sins over his head with a threat, and tells him he is too great a sinner to be saved; but Christ is able to save unto the uttermost every one that will come unto God by him.

Mr. Spurgeon used to tell the story of Mr. Brownlow North, an esteemed friend of his, but who was long a frivolous man of the world. He had been a very dissipated man, and connected with some disgraceful scenes. After his conversion he began to preach the Gospel with great fervor, and certain of his old companions were full of spite against him, probably considering him a hypocrite.

One day, when he was about to address a large congregation, a stranger passed him a letter, saying, "Read that before you preach." This letter contained a statement of certain wickednesses committed by Brownlow North, and it ended with words to this effect, "How dare you, being conscious of the truth of all the above, pray and speak to the people this evening, when you are such a vile sinner?"

North put the letter into his pocket, entered the pulpit, and after the hymns and prayer commenced his address to a crowded congregation; but before speaking on his text he produced the letter and read it to the people, and then added: "All that is here said is true, and it is a correct picture of the degraded sinner that I once was; and oh, how wonderful must be the grace that could quicken and raise me up from such a death in trespasses and sins, and make me what I am here before you to-night, a vessel of mercy, one who knows that all his past sins have been cleansed away through the atoning blood of the Lamb of God! It is of his redeeming love that I have to tell you, and to entreat any here who are not yet reconciled to God to come this night in faith to Jesus, that he may take their sins away and heal them."

Thus the attack of the enemy only gave this truly converted man the greater power to win souls to Christ. So the Savior will deal with you. He will blot your sins out of his book forever. He will cleanse the very thoughts of your heart. He will inspire your soul for holy deeds, and cause life to open before you sweeter and grander than any vision which has ever gladdened your eyes.

GALLIO THE INDIFFERENT.

"And Gallio cared for none of these things."—*Acts* xviii. 17 (Rev. Ver.).

MEN earn their title to immortality in different ways. Some live in history because of heroism, and others because of their infamy; some write their names in positive characters, and others gain a hold on remembrance because of the things they did not do. I suppose if Gallio had been told in the court-room that day that his only claim on history would be that he was the judge before whom a persecuted and hated Jewish preacher was tried, he would have laughed in contempt, but it would have been the truth. Gallio only lives to-day in human remembrance because of his relation to Paul.

Gallio does not seem to have been positively either good or bad. He was a negative character. When the Jews brought Paul before him, accusing him of blasphemy and heresy, Gallio threw the case out of court, declaring that it did not come under his province. When the Greeks took Sosthenes, the chief ruler of the synagog, and beat him in the court-room, Gallio looked on with indifference. And Luke, who made the record, says that the judge cared for none of these things. He was indifferent to the whole subject of religion. He thought his business as a judge of the law and man of the world was of infinitely more importance than all of these things which related to the worship of God and the future world. He looked upon all such subjects with contempt. And so it has happened that Gallio has come down through all the centuries as a synonym for indifference.

I think there is a good message for us in this picture. The greatest foe the Christian church has to contend with to-day is sluggishness and indifference concerning the great spiritual interests of the soul. So much of our religion is perfunctory. Men who are enthusiastic in sports, or in pleasure, or in political or business circles, become dull and heavy and sleepy, full of sluggishness and conservatism, when you talk to them about the spiritual interests of the church to which they belong, and the advancement of the kingdom of the Christ to whom they have sworn the most solemn allegiance.

One cause of this indifference must be that many people have a wrong idea of what are the best and most important things in life. Christ surely spoke with wisdom and truth when he said that where the treasure is there the heart will be also. If a man really believes that his business is much more important than his religion, then he will naturally give it a great deal more attention. If he thinks it is more important to him to stand well in his lodge than in his church, then when the lodge night conflicts with prayer-meeting or revival service, the lodge, and not the house of God, will have his presence. If people find more enjoyment in the opera or the club than they do in the church, then these seem to them the most important things, and the church service and its interests are thrust aside to receive the fag-end of their strength and attention. In saying these things I am not dealing in sarcasm at all, I am simply stating common-sense facts. A man who enjoys playing whist, or progressive euchre, or anything of that sort, more than he does the worship of God, and the seeking to be a sharer in the work of winning immortal souls to the hope that is in Christ, can not be expected to be an enthusiastic Christian. What I want to impress is, that all such people are making a great blunder as to what is the most important thing in human life; for I do maintain that the best things are not lands, or houses, or bonds, or money, or political honors, or social victories, or sensual pleasures however refined. The best things are spiritual, and have to do with one's relation to God, and Christ, and the life which does not perish. Whatever uses these worldly things have that are tempting many professed Christians away from their duty, away from their fidelity to Christ and their enjoyment of spiritual things—and that they have many uses I do not for a moment question—they possess no power in themselves to satisfy the aspirations of an immortal soul; they can not "minister to a mind diseased, nor pluck from the brain a rooted sorrow."

During the last few months some of the most cultivated people in the land—some of them elegant ladies, possessed of the highest culture, of the most brilliant social position, surrounded by all the luxuries and comforts that wealth can give, having unlimited opportunity for the pleasures which intoxicate so many giddy souls—have deliberately taken their own lives because all worldly pleasures and enjoyments had palled on the taste, and the bitterness of an empty life of vanity had eaten out their hearts, and human living had become unbearable to them. The Christian that exchanges for any worldly success or pleasure his family altar, his daily reading of the Bible, his hour of secret prayer, his attendance on revival meetings, his sympathetic and loving fellowship with Christ and his people in winning souls, is the worst-cheated man in the community. How the devil must laugh when he defrauds a man like that—gives him ashes for beautiful flowers! gives him soap-bubbles in exchange for a crown of life! gives him an hour's intoxication with the aching heart to follow, for endless peace and eternal victory!

Indifference in Christian work, especially in recommending Christ to others and seeking to win them as gems for his crown, is unworthy of us in view of the great debt which we owe Christ for our personal salvation.

At a dinner recently given by a Grand Army Post, a veteran soldier was introduced as one of the speakers. In making the introduction the presiding officer referred to the fact that the man who was to speak had lost a leg in the war, and he was naturally greeted with the most enthusiastic cheers as he rose to make his address. But he began by disavowing the introduction. "No," he said, "that is a mistake; I did not lose anything in the war; for when we went into the war we gave our country all that we had, and all that we brought back was so much clear gain."

That is the spirit of the noblest patriotism, and that is the spirit which ought to animate our hearts as the friends of Jesus Christ. He bought us with his own blood on Calvary's cross. We were the poor slaves of sin and without him we had no hope. Our acceptance of Christ was only a mockery, only a base and hypocritical ceremony, unless we gave him our whole hearts and lives; and it is unworthy of us to render him a half-hearted, sluggish, indifferent service.

The story has been told of a soldier who was missed amid the bustle of a battle. No one knew what had become of him, but his captain knew that he was not in the ranks. As soon as opportunity offered an officer went in search of him, and to his surprise found that during the battle the man had been amusing himself in a flower garden! When it was demanded what he did there, he excused himself by saying, as he hung his head in shame, "Sir, I am doing no harm." But he was tried, convicted, and shot.

Alas! That man has many a counterpart in the church of God. While we are rallying from day to day, seeking to attract sinners to hear the message of salvation, and bending all our energies to the one great work of arousing the attention of the indifferent, of presenting Christ as the One altogether lovely, many who bear the name of Jesus, and who on all occasions of dress parade are proud to be known as members of the church and friends of Jesus, are amusing themselves in the world's flower gardens, in any way which attracts their fancy. I do not speak this in anger, but with a great sense of pity for the loss that must come to any soul that misses the great opportunity of having a part in such a divine service for the Master.

Indifference to soul-saving is unworthy of the kindness of your heart, and the ordinary interest which you show in the welfare of your fellow men. You are not hard-hearted, nor lacking in the ordinary milk of human kindness. If your neighbor were starving, you would divide your last loaf with him. If a child were run over in the street before your eyes, and crushed under a heavy hoof or heavier wheel, you would be quick to offer your helpful hand and sympathetic deed.

Not long ago, in the railway depot at Nashville, Tenn., an old colored man began crying, and an excitement was raised among the travelers. The old man seemed to be in uncontrollable sorrow.

After a moment or two a depot policeman came forward and took him by the arm, shaking him roughly, and said:

"See here, old man, you want to quit that! You are drunk, and if you make any more disturbance, I'll lock you up!"

"'Deed, but I hain't drunk," replied the old man, as he removed his tear-stained handkerchief. "'I'se losted my ticket an' money, an' dat's what's de matter."

"Bosh! you never had any money to lose You dry up or away you go!"

"What's the matter yere?" queried a man as he came forward.

The old man recognized the dialect of a Southerner in an instant, and repressing his emotion with a great effort, he answered:

"Say, Mars Jack, I'se been robbed."

"My name is White."

"Well, then, Mars White, somebody has done robbed me of ticket an' money."

"Where were you going?"

"Gwine down into Kaintuck wha I was bo'n an' raised."

"Where's that?"

"Nigh to Bowlin' Green, sah, an' when de wah done sot me free, I come up dis way. Hain't ben home sence, sah."

"And you had a ticket?"

"Yes, sah, an' ober twenty dollars in cash. Bin savin' up for ten y'ars, sah."

"What do you want to go back for?"

"To see de hills an' de fields, de tobacco, an de co'n, Mars Preston, an' de good ole Missus. Why, Mars White, I'se dun bin prayin' fur it fo' twenty y'ars. Some time de longin' has cum till I couldn't hardly hol' myself."

"It's too bad."

"De ole woman is buried down dar, Mars White —de ole woman en' t'ree chillun. I kin 'member de spot same as if I seed it yisterday. You go out half-way to de fust tobacker house, an' den you turn to de lef' an' go down to de branch whar de wimmen us'd to wash. Dar's fo' trees on de oder bank, an' right under 'em is whar dey is all buried. I kin see it! I kin lead you right to de spot."

"And what will you do when you get there?" asked the stranger.

"Go up to de big house an' ax Mars Preston to let me lib out all de rest of my days right dar. I'se ole an' all alone, an' I want to be nigh my dead. Sorter company fur me when my heart aches."

"Where were you robbed?"

"Out doahs dar, I reckon, in de crowd. See! De pocket is all cut out. I'se dreamed an' pondered, I'se had dis journey in my mind fur y'ars, an' now I'se done bin robbed an' can't go?"

He fell to crying and the policeman came forward in an officious manner.

"Stand back, sir!" commanded the stranger. "Now, gentlemen, you have heard the story. I'm going to help the old man back to the old plantation and to be buried alongside of his dead."

"So am I!" called twenty men in chorus, and within five minutes they had raised enough to buy him a ticket and leave fifty dollars to spare.

When he realized his good luck the snow-haired black man fell upon his knees in that crowd and prayed: "Lord, I'se been a believer in you all my days, an' now I dun ax you to watch ober dese yere white folks dat has believed in me an' helped me to go back to de ole home."

No wonder there was not a dry eye in all the crowd of travelers that listened to the old man's prayer.

Now it seems perfectly natural to you that the old man's loneliness, his longing to go back to the old home, and die among familiar scenes, and be buried beside his friends, should have touched the hearts of those happier people and aroused them to help him. You say it would have been brutal if they could have listened to his story and been indifferent to it. But how you condemn yourself when you say that, if you are allowing days of earnest revival effort to go by without joining your prayers, your presence, and your earnest labor to help bring home those who are dying without hope and without God. All about us are men and women who have wandered away from the home of the soul, and are starving for the Bread of Life. Young men and young women by the hundreds and the thousands throng these hotels and boarding-houses about us, who were brought up in Christian homes, who were taught to pray at a mother's knee, who were told the sweet story of Christ in their childhood; but they have come out into the world and have been drawn away and enticed by its sins. The wheels of worldliness have run them down in the street and crushed them. Their highest hopes, their noblest purposes, are being smothered, and unless we shall be ready with sympathetic hand, with kindly smiles, with loving entreaty, they will be lost forever. How can you be indifferent when there is so much at stake? Think of the mothers in country homes and in little towns and villages who night after night wet their pillows with their tears as they pray for absent sons and daughters that are being tempted downward toward death and hell in this great city! What if it were your boy that was in such awful peril! What if it were your girl against whom every devilish thing seemed to be conspiring! How would you bless the pastor and the Christian men and women of a church that laid aside their business, and their social engagements, and everything else that beckoned them, and gave themselves up night after night to the great work of saving your boy or your girl! God help us to put ourselves in our brother's place, and rouse ourselves from an indifference that is unworthy of us.

But this study ought to have a message for those

of you who are not Christians, who have been indifferent to the question of your own personal salvation. You have possibly been so reared that you have been saved from the most outbreaking sins, but you have been indifferent to the claims of Christ upon your soul. The Christ who has offered to come into your heart and glorify it by his presence, has been slighted by you. You have given him no affection, no gratitude, and closed your heart against him for other guests whose presence in your heart-temple make you blush.

The great French artist Meissonier once offered to paint a picture on the white satin fan of a little girl, but the foolish little maiden said: "I just guess you won't do any such thing; I don't want my nice fan dirtied up with your old paints!" "Thus," said the great artist, "the child scorned what an empress would have prized." Has it not been thus with you? Christ has offered to come into your life and paint there the beautiful colors of love, hope, faith, patience, meekness, gentleness, and all the wondrous and beautiful conceptions of the Father's heart, and you have locked the door against him or have been indifferent to his loving offer.

When Jenny Lind returned from her American triumph, and was traveling in Italy, she went one day from Florence to the Convent of Vallombrosa, to which the young Milton went when on his travels. When she came to the chapel the monks, with courteous and deprecating regret, told her that no woman could enter.

She smiled as she said: "Perhaps, if you knew who I am, you would let me in."

"And who might the gracious lady be?" asked the monks.

And when she said, "I am Jenny Lind," every head bowed, and the doors were flung wide open.

Then, when she seated herself at the organ, and sang where Milton had sat and played, the monks crossed themselves reverently as they listened, and believed that Saint Cecilia had come back again to earth.

O my indifferent brother, if you could only know the beauty and glory of Him who craves admission to your heart, I am sure you would not remain indifferent and you would not continue to shut him out of your life! If you only knew how the music he seeks to waken in your soul would soothe your sorrows, would heal your heartaches; how it would inspire you to nobler deeds than you have dared; with what hopes of heaven it would fill your thought, and what sweet peace would fall like a benediction upon your life, you would rouse from your lethargy this very moment and let him in.

BURNING THE BRIDGES IN THE REAR.

"Many also of them that had believed came, confessing and declaring their deeds. And not a few of them that practised curious arts brought their books together and burned them in the sight of all: and they counted the price of them, and found it fifty thousand pieces of silver. So mightily grew the word of the Lord and prevailed."— *Acts* xix. 18-20 (Rev. Ver.).

PAUL was not usually a long time in a city without bringing something to pass. A common thing said about him and his companions was: "These that have turned the world upside down have come hither." The fact is that an earnest man who will preach the Gospel of Christ in its entirety in a city abounding in wickedness, is certain to run against opposition and stir up more or less excitement. Paul began to preach in Ephesus and very soon got into a collision with the soothsayers. These were, I suppose, a sort of fortune-tellers of their time. They gained their living by humbugging the people, as thousands like them do to-day. It seems to have been a great art in that day, and they had many manuscripts that were very valuable. These people came in contact with Paul, but soon found that he was more than a match for them. Paul was not alone, but was mightily endued by the Holy Spirit, so that he not only overthrew these frauds, but was given such powers of persuasion that he was able to save their souls. The exceeding sinfulness of their wicked business was brought home to their consciences with such tremendous moral force that they not only decided to quit their business, but they made public confession of their past sins, and proved the sincerity of their conduct by bringing their manuscripts, and the devices by which they had deceived the people, to the public square and making a bonfire of them. When a man so earnestly repents that he burns up ten thousand dollars' worth of the implements by which he has been getting his living, the people generally do not doubt the honesty of his purpose. No wonder there was a great excitement in the city, and that under such testimony to the power of Christ to change the heart and life the word of the Lord should be scattered abroad and widely prevail over the minds of the people. Just imagine what an excitement there would be in this city if a hundred saloon-keepers should become so convicted of the sinfulness of their business that they should call a mass-meeting on the square, and one after another stand up at the base of the soldiers' monument and confess the wickedness of their deeds and declare their purpose of getting out of the shameful business and of henceforth living Christian lives. And if then they should say that in order that you might know they had repented of their sins, and had determined on Christian lives, they would destroy the vile implements of their occupation; and then if up the street there should come the great trucks, loaded with barrels, and if, one after another, we should see these barrels of liquor emptied in the street, and their contents running in the gutter, what excitement would be caused throughout the city and how the word of God would prevail with such a testimony!

The message which I bring to you is that if you find yourself to be a sinner against God, the wisest thing you can do is to follow the example of these men of Ephesus and at once burn up the bridges behind you and thoroughly commit yourself to the Christian life. There is nothing more fatal to the character than indecision. To go on day after day feeling the pressure of duty, drawn toward it, and yet not doing it, means the gradual disintegration of will power, and the breaking down of manliness or womanliness of soul, until you no longer have the power to decide. For power of will, like other things, is a matter of habit; and it is possible to continue tampering with the will until it is destroyed. The most hopeless wrecks that drift upon the currents of life to-day are the men and women who through indecision or easy yielding to temptation have lost their self-mastery and the power to will.

A distinguished man said not long ago that an old classmate called recently at his house. He was a young man of brilliant promise and began life side by side with this man who has made such a great success. But when he came to call on his classmate the other day, he was a tramp, and had the tramp's squalor and the tramp's limp. He had slept for weeks in the lowest lodging-houses. It had come to be useless to help him; he had destroyed his power of will. His nature was like a rotten log, in which no nail would hold. His old-time friend could weep over him, he could keep him from starvation; but he could not rouse in him the power of will to save himself. Twenty years ago this poor tramp's friends said of him: "He will be a great man"; fifteen years ago they said: "He has a good deal in him"; ten years ago they said somewhat more doubtfully: "He may succeed yet"; but now they never speak of him at all; he has been drowned out of their thought, and they have lost hope for him, and the failure has been his indecision.

One may fail just as certainly of the greatest and best purposes of life and never come to be a tramp. One's moral nature, one's spiritual fiber, may come to be a rotten wall, while yet the body is delicately clothed and the physical surroundings as comfortable as ever.

These men of Ephesus were wise when they made it impossible ever to go back to their old evil trade. If they had kept those manuscripts, and there had come a time when they were out of work and had a hard time to make a living, the devil would have said to them: "What's the use of worrying? You've got the tools in the safe by which you can make money enough to live at ease." Do you not see what a tremendous lever the enemy of their souls would have had? By burning up the books they saved themselves from such temptations. Some of you need just this lesson. You are convinced that you ought to be a Christian. You are conscious that you are a sinner against God, that your life is wrong in his sight, and you have no excuse for your neglect of salvation that you would for a moment dare to offer in the blazing noonday of the judgment. And you are saying within your heart that you must do better. Certain sins about which your conscience has rebuked you, you are promising yourself, during the early days of this new year, you will forswear. But while you are thus making resolutions you are excusing yourself from making any open confession of Christ. You fail to commit yourself before your friends and associates, and you hide these good purposes within your heart as tho they were something to be ashamed of. Can you not see how frail and useless such an effort must be?

On the other hand, if you would follow the example of these Ephesians and come out openly on the Lord's side, confess Christ publicly as your Savior, bravely declare your purpose to be a Christian, you would serve notice on everybody that knows you of your change of purpose, and would be greatly strengthened and helped thereby. Such a course brings at once to your aid and support the sympathy and prayers and fellowship of all sincere Christian people. It gives you, also, a strong vantage-ground of resistance to withstand the influence of any of your associates who are not Christians who might seek to draw you back again into sin; and, above all, you have the consciousness that you are doing right and the strong fellowship of Jesus Christ to sustain and comfort and bless you in this new life of righteousness.

Possibly I speak to some who are sadly discouraged, and are almost ready to lie down in the chains of wicked habit and give up the fight. A man who is serving a twenty years' sentence in the Missouri penitentiary has refused to accept the pardon offered him by Governor Stephens. He gives as his reason for doing so that he has no friends, no money, and could find no employment, and so prefers the jail. Alas! there is many a man in bondage outside of prison walls—in bondage to wicked habits; to lusts and passions that burn the soul and blacken it with their evil fires; captured by evil imaginations; the slaves of wicked thoughts and unholy influences. Do not, I beg you, give yourself over to such a fate. So long as there is in your heart something that responds and echoes back to the song of home and heaven, there is enough of good left by which you can trust Christ and secure salvation.

Henry M. Stanley, the African hero, claims that the one virtue which has given him such conspicuous success is his strength to fight against odds when it looks hopeless. He says about himself: "No matter how near death I might be, even if I were in the hands of the executioner and surrounded by guards, I should never yield without one last desperate struggle. I should be overpowered; but what of that? I had died fighting." This may seem unreasonable, but the greatest victories in the history of mankind have been won by that kind of courage. Grant, Lincoln, Washington, Nelson, Wellington, Greely, Nansen, all had that kind of courage that would fight after the case seemed hopeless, still struggling, hoping against hope. Would to God I could arouse that sort of a feeling in any discouraged soul! You tell me you have fought against your sin and failed. I say *fight again.* Publicly confess your sins and confess your purpose to take Christ as your Savior. Do not leave out of account the mightiest factor of all—that Christ has more than human power to bring to your aid. It is no mere human voice that says to you: "Come unto me, all ye that labor and are heavy laden, and I will give you rest."

I never stand in the pulpit on Sunday evening without feeling keenly how many hopes are represented before me by young men and young women about whom distant fathers and mothers are anxious, and without a longing to be God's messenger to those who have not the shelter of the blessed home influences. I wondered the other day, when this little story came to me from Rochester, if it were one of the boys that I had shaken hands with at the church door whom his mother waited for there in the depot. The other evening, in that city, among the crowd that surged forward toward the gate as the St. Louis express rumbled into the Central depot, was a little old woman dressed in black. Jostled this way and that by the hurrying crowd, she was about to pass through the gate when the gateman stopped her by a motion of the hand and a demand for her ticket.

"I am not going away," she replied. "I didn't buy a ticket."

"Then you can't go through here. Against orders, you know."

"But, sir, my son is coming, and——"

"Can't help it," was the hurried reply. "Stay here, and he will come to you."

"Oh, sir, if he only would!" was the reply, and the tremble in the little woman's voice arrested the impatient murmur of those behind. "Oh, sir, if he only would! but he died last week, and now they are bringing him home in a coffin. He was the only one I had—oh, thank you, sir!"—The gate was thrown wide open and the sad face of the little woman in black was lost in the crowd as she went to meet her dead boy.

My heart goes out for the young men and young women who are not only away from the home fold, but are wandering away from the home Christ. How many mothers there are whose hearts are following their dear ones here with a prayer like that of the poet:

"My lamb is missing from the nightly fold,
 And bleak the wind that sweeps the darkening wold.

Where wandereth she, so late and ever bold,
        With foolish feet?
Hath any seen a lamb that's gone astray,
Caught in the hidden thorns along her way,
Or slipped a-down some steep, alack-a-day!
        With piteous bleat?

"Why to the storm is turned her tender breast?
Her fold was full of warmth and love and rest,
There was no lamb so sheltered and caressed
        The sun beneath.
Or is she housèd in an alien fold,
With simple head forgetful of the old,
And that she soon will shiver with the cold
        Upon the heath?

"Some thief hath stolen my lamb, tho many bad he,
And all the world had but this one for me.
An idle shepherd I shall ever be
        With idle crook.
There was but one I ever wished to guide
Over the chasm and up the mountainside,
Or piped to on the meadows green and wide
        From shaded nook.

"O thou Good Shepherd! seek her in the path
That many a terror, many a pitfall, hath.
On her bewildered head let not thy wrath
        From heaven break!
To the calm pastures of the Better Land,
Where all the flock are guided by thy hand
And follow only as thou dost command,
        My lost lamb take!"

O wanderers, come back to the Shepherd Christ, who follows you with gentleness and love, seeking after you that he may save. Give him now all your heart!

THE FATAL BLUNDER OF A SHREWD GOVERNOR.

"But after certain days, Felix came with Drusilla, his wife, which was a Jewess, and sent for Paul, and heard him concerning the faith in Christ Jesus. And as he reasoned of righteousness, and temperance, and the judgment to come, Felix was terrified, and answered, Go thy way for this time; and when I have a convenient season, I will call thee unto me."—*Acts* xxiv. 24, 25 (Rev. Ver.).

THE devil has no snare by which he traps so many men to their eternal despair as that of procrastination. So long as a man believes there is time enough yet to repent, that the present is inconvenient, but a time will come in the future when everything will be propitious, Satan does not need to worry about him. He feels just as sure of him as if the judgment day were already over, and he had gone away into the outer darkness.

In order to be saved, it is not enough to hear the Word of God, to be convinced of its truth, or even to be terrified because of our sins and the certain punishment they will bring. Felix experienced all that, and yet did not accept Christ. Paul preached to him and his wife the most searching gospel; he unfolded to him the glory of a righteous life, and with that mighty power which God gave to Paul as a preacher, he proclaimed to this governor, with honest words, the terrors of the judgment to come. Felix was greatly moved. He knew he was a sinner against God. His wickedness never seemed so black to him before. He shook like an aspen leaf before the picture of the just judgment that awaited his transgressions. All that Felix knew, and yet was not saved.

Some of you comfort yourselves by thinking that you can not be in any great danger of being lost, because many times you are filled with sorrow because of your sins. Your heart is yet tender, you say, and a touching song, or an incident full of pathos, will move you even to tears and fill you with a desire to be a better man or woman. Ah! thousands have felt like that, only to have their hearts grow harder and harder until they were lost forever. Dr. Wayland Hoyt tells the story of a captain whom he met in the pilot-house of a Missouri River steamboat, and the captain asked Dr. Hoyt's judgment concerning his conduct. He said when he was a young man, and was first married, his wife was a Christian, and to please her he began to go to church; he never could hear singing and not be moved; the songs they sang in the church touched him strongly. They brought up forgotten memories and unloosed the springs of feeling; he was overcome; he could not help himself, but wept whenever he went to church and heard tender songs. Because he wept, they thought he had become a Christian. His wife, the minister, and many friends pressed him to join the church. "But," said the captain, "I could not. I told them I had simply been stirred by songs as I always am. I knew I had not given up my evil ways. I knew I had not repented of my sins, and given myself over to my Savior. Tell me, was I wrong in refusing to join the church, tho songs touched me so, or right?" Dr. Hoyt wisely told him that he was right in not joining the church unless he really gave himself to Christ and repented of his sins, but that his great blunder was that he did not go on and give himself to Christ and trust Jesus to blot out his sins and lead him into a new life. Some of you are making this same blunder. Religion is not simply good impulses. It is not simply tender emotions and tearful meditations. It is decision. "Choose ye this day whom ye will serve." "Whosoever *will* may come." It is not enough to tremble, not enough to be terrified like Felix. Like the jailer at Philippi you want to cry out, "What must I do to be saved?" and, like him, accept Christ openly and decisively.

Felix made a fatal blunder in supposing that some future time would be better than the present. In the very nature of things it must get harder. Everything conspires to make this true. Habits of sin get stronger with every day's indulgence. Like the law of gravitation acting in the velocity of a falling stone, or like the current above a cataract increasing with every foot as one draws near to the awful precipice, so evil habits strengthen their deadly grip on the soul. If you can not break your habit now, what reason have you to believe you can break it after it has had time to grow stronger yet?

Another factor must be taken into account—that every added year makes it more doubtful as to whether you will ever change your habits of life. Most people who become Christians at all accept Christ in their youth. Age tends to conservatism, tends to fixedness of character, either good or ill, and you are running an awful risk in allowing the gracious influences that are about you now to pass away and leave you unsaved. God is calling you by his Spirit; if you do not yield to that influence it will be very much harder ever to move you toward a Christian life again. The scientists tell us that if you will take a little bit of phosphorus and put it on a sliver of wood and set it afire, it will give a very brilliant blaze; but, bright as the blaze is, there drops from the phosphorus a white ash that coats the wood and makes it almost fireproof afterward. And so it is when through the grace and mercy of God there has flamed up in your heart and conscience a conviction of sin. If you grieve the Spirit, if you silence your conscience, and let that illumination from heaven burn down to ashes and die out in your heart, you make it infinitely more difficult ever to kindle the light in your soul again. Do not grieve away the Spirit of God!

Some of you fully expect to seek Christ soon, but with petty apologies that are unworthy of you are excusing yourselves from accepting him as your Savior here and now. Like Felix you are saying, "Go thy way till I have a convenient season"; but, alas! that time may never come to you. The peasants of southern Russia say that an old woman was at work in her house when the Wise Men of the East, led by the star, passed on their way to go and seek the infant Savior. "Come with us," they said. "We are going to find the Christ so long looked for by men." "Not now," she replied. "I am not ready to go now; but by and by I will follow on and find him with you." But when her work was done the Wise Men had gone, and the star in the heavens which went before them had disappeared, and she never found her way to the Savior. God forbid that you should make that same blunder!

I went one night to see a woman who was dying. She knew she was dying, and in a few hours must stand before her God; but her face was all aglow with peace and joy. I prayed with her, quoting in my prayer some of the precious promises of God's Word. "Oh, the promises! Oh, the promises! how sweet and true they are!" she said. I went away, and an hour afterward, when the last moment came, her final sentence was, "For me to live is Christ, but to die is gain." A brother minister went to call on another woman who was dying. The mother of the lady met him at the door, wringing her hands in great distress. She cried out: "Oh! pray for my daughter; she is dying." The minister knelt near the bed, and tried and tried again to utter words in prayer, and could not. After struggling for a while with a strange feeling, he arose from his knees alive with the memory of what God has said: "There is a sin unto death: I do not say that you shall pray for it." As he rose to his feet the dying woman said: "I knew you could not pray for me, but I wanted to see you that I might send a message of solemn warning to my friends." After delivering this terrible message, she turned her face toward the wall, and continued to repeat the words "Too late! Too late!" until she was dead.

Which of these deaths would you prefer to die? You are making your choice, it may be, now. Thank God! it is not yet too late with you. God's call is in your ear and you have but to take him at his word to know Jesus Christ in the pardon of your sins. Now is the time to seek him. Do not let anything keep you away. The time to open the door and let your friend in is when he is knocking; Christ is now knocking at the door of your heart.

A young commercial traveler was spending the night in a hotel, and very early in the morning he heard through the thin partition separating his room from the next one the voice of a man singing. It was a hymn-tune which carried his thoughts back to his boyhood days, before he had fallen into sin. Soon the singing ceased, and the same voice was engaged in earnest prayer. The young man began to think of his own condition before God. A strong desire to pray filled his heart, but it was so long since he had prayed that he could not do so. After a few minutes he determined to ask his neighbor to pray for him. The devil tried to stop him by insinuating the thought that it was not a convenient or proper thing to do; but it seemed to the young man that it was God's call to him and he dared not let it go by. He rose, dressed rapidly, and knocked on the door of the adjoining room, and was admitted.

"What do you want?" asked the occupant, a fine old man with white hair.

"I sleep in the next room," the young man replied, "and heard you praying. I wish you would pray for me."

"Come in," was the quick response; and, closing the door, he said, "Let us kneel down." He then offered an earnest prayer for his young neighbor.

As they got up from their knees the young man was attacked with a sudden doubt as to the future, and he said: "I don't know that it is much use, my doing this, as I do not know any one in this way; and if I begin I shall not stand."

"Oh, you think you will not stand," was the answer.

"Yes," was the reply.

"Then," rejoined the old gentleman, "let us kneel down again."

They knelt down again, side by side, and the white-haired old Christian prayed in these terms: "O Lord, this young man says that he will not stand; neither will he, Lord, unless thou make him stand. Thou rememberest when, seventeen years ago, I knelt down and gave myself to thee, and thou hast kept me. Do the same for this young man, and more also; for Jesus Christ's sake. Amen."

It was the turning-point of that young man's life. He went out from that hour to live a happy, prosperous, Christian man. God help you to follow his example!

OBEDIENCE TO THE HEAVENLY VISION.

"Wherefore, O King Agrippa, I was not disobedient unto the heavenly vision."—*Acts* xxvi. 20 (Rev. Ver.).

PAUL had been educated in the law, and was well equipped to have made an eloquent and effective legal argument in the presence of King Agrippa if he had chosen so to do. But first of all, Paul was a Christian. Christ had taken possession of his life. His first and last thought about any course of conduct was: "Will it enhance the glory of Jesus Christ?" To him King Agrippa was not only a king—he was a man, a brother, one whom it was important to save as a gem for his Master's crown. Hence Paul did with him exactly as he would with the men to whom he was preaching every day—he told him his personal religious experience. Paul evidently thought that the most powerful sermon he could preach was to give his own testimony for Jesus Christ. And so, with perfect simplicity and straightforwardness, he tells Agrippa that he was a bigoted and bitter Pharisee, that he hated Christ, and persecuted the people who loved him, and sought to go to Damascus that he might, if possible, crush out all the disciples of Jesus. But as he went in the way at noon he beheld a wonderful vision of the Christ whom he had despised, and a tender voice said to him: "Saul, Saul, why persecutest thou me? It is hard for thee to kick against the goad." And Paul assures Agrippa that he was at that moment convinced of the divinity of Jesus Christ, and from that day on had given his life up in obedience to that heavenly vision.

There is a good message here for us as Christians. The most powerful lever we have by which to move the hearts of those whom we desire to see won to Christ is our own personal religious experience. If God has forgiven our sins through Christ, let us not for a moment hide our light under a bushel, but let it shine wherever we may. There is no such thing as living a happy, useful Christian life in an underhanded manner. It must be open and aboveboard. The Christ who laid aside the riches of glory in heaven and came down to bear insult and shame and poverty and death for us, standing out in the open, a target for every poisoned arrow that the hosts of hell could hurl against him, has a right to our straightforward and loyal service.

A man said to me recently that he could not understand why he was not a happier Christian. He said he knew that he had given his heart to Christ, and he felt sure that his sins were forgiven. Every night he knelt down and in sincerity thanked God for the day's mercies, and prayed God's care over him while he slept. In the morning he knelt and prayed for the divine guidance. But while the deep burden of his guilt had passed away, there was a lack of gladness and joy about his religion that he could not understand. Then I asked him if he had entered into Christian fellowship with other Christians, and he said he had not. I inquired if in the church, when opportunities were given to testify for Christ, he had stood up as a loyal friend to bear witness to the forgiveness of his sins; but he had not done that either. Then I inquired if among those who were not Christians, he had told of his faith in Christ; but that, too, he had omitted. "O man," I said, "how can you expect to have the joy of your Christian life grow into enthusiasm and inspiration while you are hiding it in the dark as something to be ashamed of? Bring the coal of fire God has given you to the family hearth where other coals are flaming, and see how brightly it will glow and shoot forth flames of gladness."

Doubtless some Christians to whom I now speak

have been making the same mistake. Your discipleship has not been open enough. Make the most notable thing about you to be that you are a Christian. Let people doubt your business opinions, doubt your politics, doubt everything else about you before they doubt that you love Jesus Christ as your Lord and Savior. If you thus honor Christ, as Paul did, other heavenly visions will come to you as they came to him. For Paul had times when he was lifted up into the third heaven, and joys and glorious visions were given him so marvelous and beautiful that he could not utter them by earthly tongue. Oh, let us come up on the mountain-top of an open, avowed consecration to Christ! With loving, devoted hearts let us sing:

> "Dwell who will in the valley below,
>   I go up into the sunshine!
> Free and warm and glad in its play,
> Light and life are in every ray,
> Burning to brighter and brighter day.
> Let who will in the valley stay,
>   I go up into the sunshine!
>
> "Mists are down in the valley below,
> Shadow and cloud wave to and fro,
> The rivers go creeping, sluggish and slow,
> The very winds have forgotten to blow.
> Dwell who will in the valley below,
>   I go up into the sunshine!

"On the golden summit the morning sings
Like a glad bird pluming his radiant wings.
The torrents flash like living things,
Sparkling and foaming the rivulet springs,
Every bright drop like a joy-bell rings.
 I go up into the sunshine!

"There in the veins the life currents flow,
The heart with fervor is all aglow,
Trumpet calls the wild breezes blow,
The soul like a warrior bold would go.
Stay who will in the valley below,
 I go up into the sunshine!"

The Christian experience of a soul made glad by the presence of Christ does good many times when we are unconscious of it. I never shall cease to thank God for an illustration I once had of that in an Eastern city. I was pastor for several years in one part of the city, and then removed to another part of the same city to take another pastorate. During my first pastorate I met almost daily, on the street, a very prominent and popular physician. He was a brilliant man and eminently successful, but not a Christian, and was rather prejudiced against Christianity. His family attended another church from my own, and I had no acquaintance with them; my only acquaintance with the man was such as you have with one to whom you lift your hat, day after day, for years. He never came to my church, never heard me preach, and I had probably never spoken two minutes with him at any one time. After I had removed to a distant part of the city, he was taken ill with a lingering disease, and tho everything was done in his behalf that wealth and the best medical counsel to be had in the land could do, he grew steadily worse until it seemed certain that he must soon die. His family became greatly interested in his spiritual condition, and he himself was terrified at what he called "the leap into the dark" which he was about to take. His wife asked if he would not like to have the pastor of the church which she attended call and talk with him, but he declined. She mentioned others, some of whom he had treated professionally, and for whom she knew he entertained respect. But he said he did not wish to see them. Finally he said: "If I could see Dr. Banks, who used to be pastor of the Methodist church here, I believe he might help me. I never heard him preach, but whenever I met him on the street I used to feel after he had passed, 'There goes a man whose religion makes him happy.'" God knows I relate this humbly and not boastfully, but I can not express to you the thanksgiving of my heart to God when they sent me his message and his reason for sending it. I went to see him at once and was able by the grace of God to lead him to open his heart to Christ. Every week for many weeks I visited him, and found him, in spite of the most terrible pain, a happy and joyous Christian man, and he died in the triumphs of his faith in Christ. Often when tempted to discouragement I have been roused by his memory to think how important it is that we be obedient to the heavenly vision which Christ has given us, and let it shine out in our faces and words, so that others who are in the darkness may see its light and be led to Christ.

But what a splendid message there is here for you who are not Christians! The essence of Paul's vision was that Jesus Christ was his Savior and his Lord, and had a right to his love and service. I am sure that some of you have that vision. Paul saw that his life hitherto had been a failure, because he had been kicking against the goad. Think of the humble illustrations used—the ox that gives his neck to the yoke and pulls loyally in his master's service is the one that has peace and reward, but the ox that kicks against his master's command has only goading and punishment. So Paul had not had a happy life in persecuting the Christians; many a bitter goading had come to him; but now he saw that Christ was his rightful master, and by taking his yoke upon him he found the yoke easy and the burden light, and found, as Christ had promised, rest unto his soul. Some of you have been making a failure in the same way. You have been going on in selfishness, refusing to Christ your rightful service, and you have had unrest; your conscience has goaded you. At the bottom of every cup of sinful pleasure you have found the bitter dregs. If you will only cease your fighting against God, and accept this vision of Christ as your Savior, you may, like Paul, enter upon a new life that shall be full of peace.

I call your especial attention to the fact that Paul found that Jesus had a right to his service, and that becoming a Christian was a perfectly natural thing to do. The devil has tried to make you believe that for you to become a Christian is something strange and unnatural, but it is not so. Sin is the invader, and to turn away from your sins with loathing and turn to Christ is like an exile coming home again. I repeat it. The most natural thing for a man to do is to repent of his sins, to cease his wrong-doing, and by the help of God begin to live the life of love and hope and faith.

The keynote of Paul's life is obedience. He was obedient to the heavenly vision. Christ says that those who keep his words—that is, those who obey him—are the ones who truly love him. So the whole question of your salvation resolves back to that one thing, Will you obey the Lord Jesus Christ? If you want to know how you may do that, you can not do better than to catch Paul's idea of it in the very next words that he spoke to Agrippa. Listen to this entire paragraph of his address: "Wherefore, O king Agrippa, I was not disobedient unto the heavenly vision: but declared both to them of Damascus first, and at Jerusalem, and throughout all the country of Judea, and also to the Gentiles, that they should repent and turn to God, doing works worthy of repentance." There it is—Repent of your sins and turn to God, doing the kind of things which are proper for a man to do who has been sinning against Christ and now repents of it. The essence of repentance is to turn unto God. Repentance is not only sorrow on account of sin, but a ceasing to sin, a turning away from sin, and beginning to do the things that will please Christ. When we come to that, we know that nothing save an open confession of Christ can possibly please him or ought to please him.

How glad you ought to be that here in the midst of health and strength, with some opportunity to work for the Lord and show the genuineness of your repentance and your love for him, you may make such a confession. The physician of whom I spoke a moment ago had only one regret in all those last weeks of his life, and that was that he could not live long enough to show his gratitude and love for Christ. He used to say to me: "Oh, if I could only have back again the strength and health of which I was so prodigal, that I might use it to make everybody know how generous Christ has been to me, how great his love to save me who was so great a sinner; how gladly I would spend all my time and strength in his service." Such an opportunity could not come to him, but that blessed privilege is yours. You may accept Christ now. You may be obedient unto his commands, and have the joy of so serving him that multitudes may be led to Christ and his salvation through your obedience to the heavenly vision

THE SNARE OF THE SOFT SOUTH WINDS.

"And when the south wind blew softly, supposing that they had obtained their purpose, they weighed anchor and sailed along Crete, close in shore. But after no long time there beat down from it a tempestuous wind."—*Acts* xxvii. 13, 14 (Rev. Ver.).

PAUL had urged most strongly against this voyage, but the owner of the vessel and the captain thought they knew a great deal more about the sailing of a ship than any preacher, and so, when the sun shone with encouragement and the soft south winds were balmy, they laughed at Paul's warning and set out on their way with gay hearts. They had not gone very far, however, before they found out their mistake. The wind switched about, and was soon beating upon them in the fury of a tempest. The soft south winds had been so propitious and the weather so promising that they had gone in close to the shore, taking chances that they would never have thought of risking in a storm. They would have given anything now for more sea-room, but the ship was caught in the tempest and driven helplessly before the wind.

The special lesson which I wish to impress is the danger of being deceived by the soft south winds of prosperity and ease, which may be fanning your cheeks at the present time. A human life has its climatic changes, like the weather on the Mediterranean Sea; that the weather is fair to-day, and the wind blowing softly from the south, is no sign that it will continue so to-morrow, but rather an indication that it will not, for the weather is liable to change, and storms are certain to come ere long.

Many young people are led to think lightly of the necessity of building up a strong and solid character, because life seems to them like a sunny sail on sheltered waters, with only soft south wind enough to make the voyage pleasant. They have been so hedged about by father and mother and friends, and so inspired by the natural buoyancy of youth and health, that it is hard for them to believe their sea—the sea on which they sail with such exultant hearts—may soon be swept by a fierce and bitter tempest and their frail boat caught and driven by the storm, and in danger of eternal shipwreck.

Yet it is not well for us to be thus deceived. Every one of us must stand the storms of life, and it is worse than foolish—it is wicked—not to be making preparation for them. A wise shipbuilder does not build his vessel for the calmest weather that is likely to be met, but he keeps in his mind the fury of the roughest storm. The ship will, of course, have many calm days, many days when sailing is only a pleasure, and when the winds in no sense test the capacity of the ship; but the shipbuilder who is master of his business keeps in mind the tempest which is likely to come at any time. He knows that any boat can make a good showing in fair weather, but the true test of the vessel's ability comes out in the time of storm.

And so it is with a man or a woman. So long as we are young and strong, our friends are kind, good fortune favors us, and the soft winds of prosperity fill our sails, there is no way to tell what we are capable of doing. No man really knows himself so long as the winds and currents of life are with him; it is when he has to make his way in the teeth of the gale—when health fails, or money is lost, or his friends desert him, and all his plans are awry; it is when the thunder of threatened ruin rolls over his head, and lightning flashes of strife and sorrow and wretchedness throw a baleful light over his storm-swept deck, revealing his tattered sails—it is only then that a man comes to know the metal that is in him. When everything is prosperous and the sea is smooth as a sheet of paper, the tide propitious, and the south wind soft, any skiff will float in safety; but the man who rides the sea in a hurricane wants solid oak between him and the boiling waves.

Let no one be deceived. However peaceful and quiet your life may have been up to this time, there are storms which you must face in the future, and no one can tell how soon they may beat upon you. It is not whether you can do without the righteousness of God now; can you do without him in the time of storm and struggle, when everything that is for you now will be against you? You must remember that every element of life with which you deal is uncertain. You say: "Well, there's one thing sure, I am young and strong, and nobody can take that from me." Alas! there is nothing so fragile and uncertain as the vigor of health and the strength of youth. People as strong and well as you are to-day have been laid on a sick-bed in less than a month's time to endure through months and years the agony of pain. Or some shadow like blindness may fall upon your life without warning, and leave a pall that never can be lifted. I remember at this moment a young man for whom I labored earnestly for many months, seeking to persuade him to give the fervor and freshness of his young manhood to Christ. He was a very engaging young man, with every sense and faculty alert and keen, and the consciousness of his youth and strength was a great delight to him; and he would say to me: "I will seek Christ after a while. I expect to become a Christian, but I am very young yet, and there can surely be no hurry for one so young as I." One day he came home through the heat, not feeling well, and the next day he was worse. In a few days he complained that he did not see clearly; in a month he could no longer see to read; in two months sight had died out. More than a year has now passed, and he is hopelessly blind. God in his mercy has spared his life, and he has given himself to Christ, and he who is the Light of the world is to-day the great comfort of his heart. All the things that once comforted him have passed out of his reach.

So it is with money, and your power to earn it. And your friends, who are the very bulwark of your life as it seems to-day, are all subject to sickness, to change, and death. Ah! the very elements are full of storms for you.

I do not say these things to discourage you or make you sad. I say them because they are true, and it is infinitely important that you should recognize them, and not go to sea in a leaky vessel, without a chart or a compass or a pilot, for your sea will certainly be swept by the storm, and you will need to see that your character is built of sterling righteousness; that your chart and compass are as true as the Word of God; and that Jesus Christ is the Pilot and the Captain of your ship.

Your ship may be said to be your principles, the solid structure on which you live and do business day by day. Ask yourself now the solemn questions: "Is my ship of principles all right? Is it pleasing to God? Does it deserve to weather the storm?" The other day a young man gave me as his excuse for not becoming a Christian that he could not be a Christian in his business. He said it was impossible in the confidential position which he held. He declared that his employer demanded of him that he should misrepresent things, and deal dishonestly, and that he would lose his place if he were to undertake to live a Christian life. I told him he had better a thousand times lose his place than go on doing what he knew was not right. That young man, and every young man like him, may go on waterlogged for a while, but it is a leaky ship, and is certain to go to bottom in the end. How glad I was to hear another young business man say that when he could not succeed in business and be honest toward God and man, he would quit the business and stand faithful to God. That is the only safe course, and a man who will stick to that has under him a ship that can face the teeth of the gale. A man with that kind of a ship has a chart and compass that can be relied upon. The Bible is the one sure chart of human life. The men who have turned away from it, however shrewd and cunning they may have been, however rich in the treasures of the world, have run on the rocks in the end; but no man ever yet took God's Word for his counsel, and directed his life by it day by day, and came to failure.

To such a ship Jesus Christ comes as Pilot and Captain, and when he is on board nobody need fear the waves, for he is Lord of the waves. Do you remember that night on the Sea of Galilee?—a sudden storm had come up, and the friends of Jesus were in the midst of it, ready to perish, and Christ came walking to them on the waves; and they were filled with fear at the sight of him and thought it was a ghost, when he spoke in loving assurance, "Lo, it is I! be not afraid." And when he came into the vessel and spoke to the troubled waters they soon came to the land with peace and safety. So Christ is willing to come to you. He will repair your ship. He will build it anew on a keel of righteousness as solid as the eternal hills. He will stay with you when the south winds blow softly and when the tempests rage. He knows all the coast line of your human life. Not a treacherous rock, or a dangerous current, or a sand-bar stretching across the channel but he knows it well. He is not a captain without experience. The Captain of our salvation was made perfect through suffering. He has undergone all our temptations, and stood all the storms of human life, but has always come off victorious.

In addition to all the danger of shipwreck that may come to you from the outside, so long as you are a sinner against God you carry within your own heart the elements of disaster and destruction. News has come recently of a most terrible fire in Baku, on the shores of the Caspian Sea. It is a strange region there. Everything seems saturated with oil; the air one breathes is laden with the odor. Not only is black naphtha to be seen in monster fountains, but white naphtha flows of itself in places. Everything is saturated—all round between the wells lie lakes of seething naphtha; the roads have naphtha streams by the sides. And it only took one rashly thrown match to set miles in a blaze with an awful conflagration. A man who is a sinner against God, and who is hiding down under the hatches of his life wicked ambitions, selfish indulgences, evil purposes, rebellious thoughts against Christ, carries in his own nature the elements of combustion that only require some devil's match of evil temptation to set his soul on fire to his ruin.

Remember this, that no man is safe unless he is genuinely and sincerely good, and that no man can be truly good in the sight of God unless he yields his life in obedience to the will of God. Are you doing that? If not, are you willing to do that now? Will you now turn from your sins and accept Jesus Christ as your personal Savior?

Christ is seeking for you now. Dr. Horton, of London, tells of a Scotchman who had been in an evangelistic meeting up in a Highland town, and had been deeply moved. He longed to find Christ, and he left the church with his whole heart set upon that. As he went down the steps into the street a poor old woman just ahead of him slipped and fell. His heart was tender, and he came up to her and said, "Do take my arm and let me help you." The old woman said to him: "You must be one of the Lord's bairns or you would never offer your arm to an old woman like me." He said, "No, I am not; but I am seeking"; and the old woman said: "All right, for when there be two seeking there is sure to be a finding."

Christ is always seeking after men and women with infinite love. All through these long years since he died upon Calvary's cross, he has been seeking after lost men and women as a shepherd seeks after the wandering sheep lost in the mountain cañons and in danger of being devoured by the wolves. All through the years of your life since first you strayed from the innocency of your babyhood, he has been seeking you. He is seeking you now. Even tho you have thrust him away, and taken the tiller of your life-ship in your own hands, until in your folly the storm gathers about you and you are threatened with wreck, even now he comes through the darkness of the storm and is saying to you, "Lo, it is I! be not afraid."

THE EMPHATIC DATE IN HUMAN LIFE.

"To-day if ye shall hear his voice, harden not your hearts, as in the provocation."—*Heb.* iii. 15 (Rev. Ver.).

THE emphatic date in a human life is *to-day*. Yesterday is beyond our reach as certainly as tho a thousand years had intervened. To-morrow may never come to us; or if it comes, it will be mortgaged by duties of its own. To-day is where God puts the emphasis of life, and where we should put it. This is true especially because what we are doing day by day is dictating destiny for the future. It is well to notice with care the special reason which Paul gives for heeding the call of Christ to-day. It is because we are in danger of hardening our hearts so that the heavenly call will no longer have any effect. History and observation alike prove that Paul is correct in that fear. There is a hardening influence about sin, and it is impossible to pursue an evil course without being hardened in the conscience by the very recurrence of the habits we indulge.

Many a young man going out from a **pure Chris-**

tian home where his teaching has been full of reverence toward God and purity of speech, has felt loathing and a distinct shock to his moral nature on hearing profane language. But if he has gone on with such associations, he has been astonished, after a little, to find himself becoming so accustomed to hearing the name of God profaned that it no longer awakens even a serious protest in his mind and heart. A young man talking to me on this subject not long ago, said that he was reared in a Christian home where he had always treated God's name with reverence, and that after he went to live away from home, he well remembered the first time a profane oath crossed his lips. He was shocked and abashed to the very heart. A flush of shame burned on his cheek and his eyes filled with tears as he thought how horrified his mother would be if she knew of his profane speech. His conscience, too, was aroused, and for a time he guarded himself; but not being a Christian it was not long before the power of evil association told upon him, and he swore again. The second time the revolt was not so great, and so he went on until he acquired the silly, wicked habit, and until he would take the name of God in vain unconsciously, not knowing that he had done so. His heart had hardened on the subject until his very spirit had become irreverent.

Other sins have the same effect, and there is no sin that men commit, if persisted in, that will not steadily harden the heart until the sinner will no longer be keenly alive to the deadly character of sin. Isaiah says, "Wo unto them who call evil good, and good evil." If a man harden his heart and sear his conscience as with a hot iron by continuing in sinful habits, there will come a time when he will do the evil and scarcely know that it is evil.

One may harden the heart in listening to the Gospel while yet refusing its gracious influence. The blacksmith hardens iron by melting and cooling it again and again, and so a man may harden his heart by resisting the convictions of sin that are aroused in his conscience by hearing the Gospel. That hardening process has already gone on to a perilous point in some of you. A man said to me since this series of meetings began: "I know that I am a sinner against God. I know that I ought to be a Christian. I am convinced that I should confess Christ, but it would be folly to start without more feeling on the subject than I have now. I have not so much feeling as I have had at other times." Alas! he probably never will have as much feeling as he has had at other times. The time was when God strongly moved upon his conscience, when his heart was melted down before the tenderness and gentleness of Christ, when he shed tears because of his sin, and the Holy Spirit mightily strove with him to bring him to repentance. But he refused the divine call. He grieved away the Spirit of God. He threw himself into wordliness and sin that his emotions might be cooled down so that they should not disturb him, and he has succeeded far too well. He has hardened his heart against the message of God's mercy. Have not some of you done the same thing? There was a time when you were very easily moved on the subject of religion. You can remember when you could scarcely hear read or told the story of Christ's being crowned with thorns, or nailed to the cross, without your heart being tenderly touched and melted down at the thought of his love for you; but now you can hear these things almost unmoved. What are you going to do? Will you go on and on, letting your heart get harder and harder still, until it is like adamant, and your face is set like a flint toward ruin? God forbid!

To-day is important because every day that is spent in indecision or in rejection of Christ strengthens in your heart the cord of rebellion that holds you away from Christ. Once there was an overladen coal-barge on the Ohio River. One morning a sailor came to the captain and told him that the water was gaining upon the vessel, but the captain was a dictatorial, wicked man, and drove him away with an oath. The faithful man came again and again with his warning, but each time he was unheeded. Finally the barge began to give undoubted evidence of being in a sinking condition. The captain ordered the men to the boats. They took their places. He then said, "I told you there was plenty of time," and took his huge knife to cut the cable which bound the boat to the barge. But he fell back with a cry of horror. The cable, instead of being a rope, was an iron chain! So the slight resistance to Christ caused by timidity or misunderstanding, which was only a small cord in your boyhood or girlhood and could easily have been overcome, as the years go on comes to be an iron cable strongly fastened in the sins of your daily life.

A very strong illustration is suggested in the last four words of the text—"as in the provocation." The reference is to the manner in which the Israelites hardened their hearts against God and provoked him in the wilderness, and for their sin failed at the last to enter the Promised Land. Once they were at the very door of the land of Canaan, the land of abundance, and Moses sent the spies over; and when they came back they all brought one story about the beauty of the country.

They all agreed that it was fertile, that it flowed with milk and honey and abounded in grapes and corn. Caleb and Joshua, young men of decision who trusted God, urge that they go up at once and possess the land, trusting in the power of God to make the conquest. But the others were afraid. They had caught sight of some giants, and declared to Moses that they were no match for these people, and that if they started in to possess the Promised Land they would be driven out in disgrace and shame, or utterly destroyed. The result was that for forty years they wandered in the wilderness, suffering hardships indescribable, and finally all died without another sight of Canaan, except Caleb and Joshua, the two young heroes who had dared to believe God.

Some of you are talking like the spies who were afraid of the giants. You want to be a Christian. You are thoroughly convinced that a true Christian life is the happiest life in the world, and you feel that you would give anything if you could be at peace with God and know that your life was pleasing to Christ; but you imagine there are such giants in the way that you fear to start lest you falter and be overcome and drop out by the wayside. Thus you are hardening your hearts and losing the blessed opportunity which, it may be, will never come to you again.

Do not forget that it is your very salvation which is at stake. It is the day of *salvation* that Paul is speaking about. You are in danger. Salvation means that there is something to be saved from. Your sin against God is not merely a blunder, or a mistake; it is not merely a question of taste; it is a crime which must be punished unless forgiven through your penitence and faith in Jesus Christ. Salvation means that you are in peril, and that you need, above all things, a refuge where you may hide your guilty soul from punishment. You can not stand on your own merits, for you would be the worst witness that could be called at the judgment. You would be forced to admit that you were a sinner against God, and out of your own mouth you would be condemned. Your own memory and your own conscience would be all the witnesses it would be necessary to call to make your condemnation sure. Your wicked deeds are all treasured up. Sometimes you forget your sin for a long time. Conscience seems to be drugged, and sleeps heavily, giving you little or no disturbance; but when you think your sin is buried the deepest, suddenly, like a flash of lightning out of a clear sky, the death of a friend, or the sudden sinfulness of a neighbor, or a shaft from God's Word uncovers your heart and your sin stares you in the face as fresh and alive as ever. Ah! there will be no lack of witnesses at the great assize. There is only one way to get rid of your sins, and that is to have them forgiven; to have them blotted out in the atoning blood of Jesus Christ. How tenderly God's Word calls you to salvation. By every possible illustration God seeks to make the invitation gracious and kindly. Hear Jesus saying: "As a hen gathereth her brood under her wings, but ye would not." And long before that the voice of the Psalmist declared: "He shall cover thee with his pinions, and under his wings shalt thou take refuge." Did you ever see the little chickens, pursued by a hawk, run at the cry of alarm from the mother hen, and hide themselves under her wings? So God is calling you at this hour to fly to the wings of his love and find refuge.

But that means action on your part. Action now. The hawk is in the air above you. If the wing of Christ's love is to be your refuge, you must fly to it at once. In the old days in Israel, when a man was out on the hills with the avenger of blood pursuing at his heels bent on taking his life, there was only one way to safety, and that was to fly with haste until he put the walls of the City of Refuge between him and his pursuer. O gather up all your powers now, and haste to put the blood of Jesus Christ between you and your sins! The call is now. The emphasis is on to-day. The opportunity will soon pass, but salvation may be yours if you will act now.

Once in a fire in New York city, a fireman of a hook and ladder company was at the top of a swaying ladder, which fell short by a whole story of a fifth-floor window from which a terror-stricken woman was leaning. Fire and smoke were behind her, and there was no time to descend and get a longer ladder. The heroic fireman twisted one leg about the top rung of the ladder, and, supporting himself with his other leg, leaned out at a sharp angle. This required great strength. The ladder swayed fearfully.

"Jump!" shouted the fireman.

There was no time to wait on the decision. Had the woman waited a single moment her fate would have been sealed; but she did not hesitate. Like a flash of lightning she saw her chance and took it. She jumped from the window and the fireman caught her. There was an instant when this sudden addition of weight made the escape of both from an awful fall a fearful improbability. Then the man's nerve and strength came to the rescue. Slowly he recovered his balance and carried the woman down the ladder amid the cheers of applauding thousands.

Jesus Christ, your Savior, has made of his own body nailed to the cross a ladder over which you may climb from peril to salvation. No one ever yet has been lost who trusted all to him, but tomorrow may be too late. To-day is yours. To-day is the day of salvation. "If ye hear his voice, harden not your hearts, as in the provocation."

THE SQUANDERED BIRTHRIGHT.

"Esau, who for one mess of meat sold his own birthright."—*Heb.* xii. 16 (Rev. Ver.).

Esau was a bright young fellow. He had many attractive qualities. He was open-handed and generous in his ways, fond of outdoor sports, liked to hunt, and was the kind of a person that is apt to be popular on all sides. But many a brilliant young man has made a sad outcome of life because of the same fatal poison that lurked at the heart of Esau.

Esau cared far more for present comfort and enjoyment than for the building up of a strong character and preparing for a permanently successful career. He could not do without his dinner, but he could get along without the blessing of God. The sin of Esau did not begin that day when he came home from the hunt, having had bad luck and taken no venison, tired out, and hungry as a famished wolf. It had begun a good while before that. The fact was, that he cared very little about his birthright. Altho his father was a good man who lived a life of prayer and honor, Esau seems to have been given up to physical enjoyment. To eat and drink and be merry, to spend his days in the wild freedom of the hunt, to deny himself no sort of physical indulgence that tempted —that was Esau's idea of a good time. His appetite for meat was a great deal stronger than his love for truth and honor. He held it to be a little thing that he was the son of one of God's princes. He had gotten out of sympathy with the prayerful spirit of his father's house, and had come to the point where he regarded his birthright lightly, and thought he had well sold it when he got a pot of meat for it.

The question for us to answer is, "What are we doing with our birthright?" for the appetites of the flesh are as dangerous temptations to-day as they were in the days of Esau. On every side of us are multitudes who are selling their birthright to clean bodies and pure hearts, their birthright to fellowship with Jesus Christ and a hope of heaven, for the physical indulgences of an hour.

In Chile, among the Andes Mountains, the Government has been paying a large bounty for the destruction of condors, as these fierce birds preyed on the herds of cattle. The method of destroying them is very interesting. A dead horse or cow is placed on the plain at the foot of a mountain, where it can be easily seen from all points. After placing their bait, the hunters set up their tents and the canvas flies that conceal them and their horses from the view of the condors. Very soon, from their peep-holes in the canvas, they see the condors coming down through the clouds, from the mountain crests, straight toward the bait. They wait patiently until a dozen or more of the birds have eaten heartily of the meal provided for them, and then they spring to their horses, which stand ready, bridled and saddled, for the chase. In a moment they are off, lariats in hand, after the condors. Now when a condor has gorged itself it can not rise for flight until it has run a long distance to give itself momentum. The hunter's method is to follow the birds for half a mile or more, and then as they rise to throw the lariats over their heads. An expert lassoer can send his rope over a condor's head and so manage it that it slips down until it touches the shoulders of the wings before it tightens on the bird. The condor is then a prisoner, but able to use his powerful pinions, breathe freely, and lead the horseman a wild chase across the plain, turning in all directions in his frantic flight, but unable to rise higher than the length of the lasso. When the rider tires of the sport, or the bird becomes sufficiently weakened, he turns the horse about and leads the chase himself, forcing the unwilling bird along until it falls, spent, to the ground, and is dragged to death at the horse's heels.

It is thus that the devil lassoes men and women. Men and women created for noble deeds, and endowed with possibilities of soul flight in a lofty spiritual atmosphere, with ability to rise in the face of the Sun of Righteousness, and rejoice in fellowship with the good and pure of earth and heaven, squander their holy birthright, and, captured by their fleshly appetites and lusts, lose their power to soar above the earth. Is it not true that during this series of meetings some of you, convicted of your sin, have sought to break away and fly aloft toward Christ your Savior? But you have felt the devil's lasso of some evil habit tighten about your neck, and your wings have beaten, as it were, the empty air. There is One who is able to cut that awful lariat that holds you. Jesus Christ can make you free, and whom the Son of God makes free is free indeed.

Many times a man's birthright of innocency and hope passes out of his possession so gradually that he does not realize the awful loss until it is beyond recall. If at the beginning of any course of sin a man had the whole question thrust before him, and knew how much was at stake, he would start back in horror.

A curious case is puzzling the doctors in one of

the Brooklyn hospitals. It is that of a man whose hair turned white in a night. When he went to bed in the evening, his hair was brown. When he awoke in the morning and looked at himself in the glass, he staggered with surprise, and well he might, for his hair and eyebrows were white as snow. The physicians could make nothing of the case, but conjectured that he had been poisoned with some materials in which he had worked. If a man were tempted suddenly to turn from good to bad like that, he would start back in loathing. If the young man of twenty, full of the vigor and strength of his young manhood, were invited suddenly, in a single hour, to become a drunkard with blear eyes and blotched face, bloated body and shattered nerves, he would start back in horror at such a proposition. No young man in the land is fool enough to sell his physical birthright at one auction like that, but the devil works insidiously. It is only a single glass of sparkling wine that tempts, and all the miserable outcome is hidden in the maze. Men go down into wicked habits by such easy gradations that they are shocked at nothing until they find themselves lost in the mire.

O my young friend, hear me when I make the heart-searching inquiry, Are you selling your birthright by piecemeal? Be sure that if you have in any way mortgaged your soul to Satan, the time will come when with merciless cruelty he will foreclose that mortgage.

Paul declares to the Philippians that our rightful citizenship is in heaven. We were born the sons of God. It is an awful thing to count that citizenship a little thing and squander it on passing pleasures that will soon turn to bitter dregs. It is a great thing to be the citizen of a country with a strong government back of you, able to defend you. When the present Cuban insurrection broke out, Dr. Alberto Diaz, one of the most successful Christian missionaries in the world, was arrested at his home in the city of Havana, thrown into prison, and sentenced to be shot the next morning. At evening two coffins were brought in and placed in his sight. One was for himself, and one for his brother John, who was in prison with him. The two brothers, when they saw the coffins, fell on each other's neck and wept a little, but soon wiped away their tears, saying: "Others have died for Jesus; why not we? So let us die like men!"

With this conclusion they went to sleep. In the middle of the night the soldier who was marching back and forth, keeping the death-watch, came to Alberto Diaz, woke him up by gently kissing his hand, and said in a vigorous whisper: "Pastor! pastor! I'm not a Spaniard. I'm a Cuban, and a member of your church. I got myself put on guard here to-night that I might save your life. Tell me how to do it!"

Diaz sat up, rubbing his eyes, and said: "Well, if you're what you say you are, get me a pencil and paper."

The soldier did so.

Diaz wrote a telegram and said, "Get this into the hands of my wife."

His wife sent it to Atlanta, Ga. From Atlanta a telegram went to the Secretary of State at Washington. He cabled to Madrid, and from Madrid a cablegram went back to Havana saying "Don't shoot Diaz. He is an American citizen. Banish him." All this in a few hours' time.

So it was worth something; it was worth the man's life to be an American citizen. It is worth eternal life to be a citizen of the kingdom of heaven, to be a joint heir with Jesus Christ to an inheritance that is incorruptible and full of glory!

Last autumn there was a good deal said in the newspapers about a scheme to purchase Thomas Jefferson's famous home in Monticello and make of it a public reservation; but the plan was thwarted at the very start by the refusal of its owner, Mr. Jefferson M. Levy, a descendant of the great commoner, to part with it. He said, when asked about the project, that it was a matter of personal and family pride with him that Monticello be kept up, and that no sum of money could possibly compensate him for the loss of the estate. Some years ago, William M. Evarts, then Secretary of State, urged Mr. Levy to allow him to ask Congress to purchase Monticello. His answer was: "Mr. Secretary, if you offered me all the money this room would hold, you could not tempt me." Mr. Evarts replied: "Well, Mr. Levy, I admire you, and do not blame you."

There is something in every true, generous heart that responds to such fidelity to a noble family inheritance. But how much more precious is your inheritance as the son or the daughter of God—the privilege of communion with your heavenly Father; the right to dwell at peace, assured of his divine protection, knowing that all things work together for your good because his arms are about you; the privilege of walking arm-in-arm in sweet yoke-fellowship with Jesus Christ, your Savior, the one altogether lovely character in human history. And yet if you persist in your sin you forfeit all that, you squander that divine birthright. And what do you get in return? A morsel of meat, with the aching heart, the scorpion whip of the conscience, and the ages of remorse to follow. I am sure that your reason and every noble impulse of your soul cry out against such prodigality.

Ah, but, you say, it is already too late. I have squandered my birthright. I have already gorged myself in wicked indulgence, the lasso of evil habit is already around my neck, and I am being dragged at the heels of my captors. Oh, I thank God that even in so sad a plight I may bring you a message of hope. Jesus Christ, your Savior, who died on the cross to redeem you, passes this way with love in his heart, a pardon in his hands, and will, if you will accept him, set you free from your pitiable condition. Do not refuse an offer so gracious, or turn your back on a freedom so sweet!

THE LORD'S BROTHER.

"James, the Lord's brother."—*Gal.* i. 19 (Rev. Ver.).

THIS particular James was the son of Joseph and Mary, and grew up in the home of the carpenter in Nazareth, and had, no doubt, played among the shavings in the little carpenter shop with Jesus. He was the brother of the Lord. We do not know just when he became, also, one of the disciples of Christ. From the record that is given us of Christ's first sermon at Nazareth, where the people sought to kill him by throwing him over a precipice, we know that his brothers were still at home and James had not yet joined him. We are surely not astonished that a young man who had grown up in fellowship with such a brother as Jesus must have been should have been lonely at home without him, and should have early craved the privilege of following him and sharing his fate.

It is this striking phrase, the brother of the Lord, and the deep and holy meaning that is breathed from it for our help, which I desire that we shall study together. We can imagine with what loving reverence the men of that little band of Jesus's friends would naturally speak of one who could be called by such a sacred name as the brother of the Lord. Surely James could never have heard himself called by this name without feeling the great honor which was done him, and without deep humility. He must often have felt unworthy of it when he reflected with sorrow that he had held back while even strangers were giving their love and allegiance to his brother, and had not been the first to become his true and loyal disciple. And so I think any one of us who should hear himself called the brother of Jesus—and surely every Christian man who is giving loyal service to Christ has a right to be so called—must be filled with humility at such an honor as he looks back over the unworthiness of his past life. But, thank God! past sins do not make it impossible for us at the present time to be in deed and in truth the brothers and sisters of the Lord. Jesus is so great in the breadth of his charity and love that not only can he forgive his open enemies, but he can do what most of us find so much harder —forgive the desertion of friends on whom he has heaped the evidences of his love.

Now let us, every Christian, think of ourselves as bearing this title. How should I live who am to stand before the world as the Lord's brother, or the Lord's sister? Paul went up to Jerusalem an entire stranger to all the Christian people there. They were, no doubt, very curious to see him. His bitter persecution of the Christians, his presence at the death of Stephen, his remarkable conversion—all this would make him a marked character; and when he came to visit Peter, Peter introduced him to James, and no doubt used this expression which Paul quotes. Let the picture come back before you: Paul comes as a visitor. Peter and James are in a room together. Paul is admitted, and Peter, the leading, masterful spirit of the disciples, comes forward and receives Paul lovingly, and then turns about and with a reverent tone almost like a caress he says to Paul, "This is James, the Lord's brother."

Now I want to ask very earnestly, How much must it have meant for James himself, in his own watchfulness over his conduct and spirit and life, to be constantly regarded and continually presented to strangers as the brother of Jesus Christ? It surely could not have failed to give him a very keen sense of responsibility for maintaining the honor of Jesus. In James's case it involved the good name of the family, the reputation and standing of everything that was dear to his heart. Why should it not be so with us? We have been redeemed by the blood of the Lord Jesus Christ.

He has sought after us as poor lost sinners, and has knocked at the door of our hearts until we have opened them to his coming, and in the truest and noblest sense we are the brothers and sisters of Jesus Christ. Surely if our divine Lord is not ashamed of us, and is willing to call us his brethren and to trust his good name in our keeping, we ought to accept the term at once with humility and a deep and holy joy.

The next thought, however, is very startling, but the logic will not be refused when once we have come thus far in our thinking. It is that men and women are forming their opinions of Jesus by what they see in us. The name of the whole family of Jesus Christ, in heaven and in earth, is committed as a sacred trust to you and to me for our keeping. There can be no more solemn question than this: "How am I keeping that sacred trust? Am I justifying the confidence that Jesus reposed in me when he called me to be his brother or his sister?"

I am sure that it is a sad reflection to many of us that our representation of Christ is often so imperfect, that many times when we are prosperous and happy in a temporal and worldly way we are so forgetful of the Lord and do not show forth his spirit so much in those glad days which we owe to his love as we do when the hard hand of discipline and trouble gets hold upon us and crushes out the perfume which is latent in our hearts. It seems to me a pathetic thing that God should so often be compelled to crush our lives in order to save our souls. How much more grateful and beautiful it would be if we would live worthy of the brotherhood of Jesus Christ and of the sweet gifts he has bestowed upon us, and show forth in health and strength and prosperity the full blossoming of the Christian graces.

There is a recent invention in gathering perfume that is very interesting. If you have given the matter attention, you are aware that heretofore the only method of extracting the perfume of flowers has been the ugly way of crushing them and cooking them in beef fat; but a man in San Diego, Cal., who has been experimenting with flowers and perfume for a good many years, has studied out a new method of collecting the sweet odors, by which he gets the fragrance without destroying the flower. The instrument which he has invented is carried into a greenhouse and placed among the flowers whose odors it is desired to collect. The vapor which rises from the flowers is filled with their fragrance, and as it meets the surface of the glass funnel of his new instrument, it is condensed into drops and trickles down into the receiver. It is thought that this will revolutionize the gathering of perfumes throughout the world. If we would do the will of God perfectly, yielding our hearts with fidelity and devotion to Jesus Christ as our Savior and our Lord, receiving our joys from him as reverently as we do our sorrows, seeking both in joy and sorrow so to bear ourselves that we shall bring honor to our divine Lord, I am sure he would be able to gather the sweet perfume our lives should yield without spoiling the outward beauty of the flower.

The difficulty with so many of us is that our testimony for Christ is so irregular. At times we are good witnesses, and on other occasions poor ones. We glorify the Lord sometimes, and at other times we libel him. Such irregularity in our conduct can only come from a sad lack of continuous devotion to the Lord in our hearts. If we are constantly true to Christ there will be no barren places in our lives, but his promise to the woman of Samaria at the well of Sychar will come true, and the water which he shall give us will not be subject to drought, but will be in us a well of living water, pure and abundant, springing up into everlasting life.

Prof. Baldwin Spencer, a naturalist who has been recently making explorations in central Australia, informs us that in that land one often travels mile after mile over bare, stony plains, with scarcely a sign of plant or animal life. The sun beats down hotly on shining fields of brown and purple stones. That is in the drought time. But when the rainy season comes, everything is transformed. Clay pans and water holes will become noisy in a single night with the croaking of frogs; crustaceans hatch out with wonderful rapidity from eggs which have lain on the dry ground for, it may be, many months; small mollusks buried in clay are released, and every inhabitant of land and water revels in the joy of living. The ground within a day or two is green with the leaves of countless seedlings, which grow rapidly; birds appear as if by magic, and the once dry and silent country is now bright with flowers and foliage and animals, all decked out in their liveliest colors.

Like that dry and burned-up desert land with its shimmering stones in the heat and drought is an individual Christian or a church that has been given over to formality and worldliness until every green hope has withered, until real reverence has been strangled in forms, until enthusiastic love and brotherliness have been smothered in selfishness and pride, and life—beautiful, joyous life—has died out in sound and coloring. But when such a soul or such a church is drawn back from indifference and begins like the prophet of old in the land of Ahab to pray for rain; when in penitence and faith the heart is turned toward Christ, longing for the coming of the Lord and for his presence, and crying aloud with the Psalmist: "As the hart panteth after the water brooks, so panteth my soul after thee, O God. My soul thirsteth for God, for the living God: when shall I come and appear before God? My tears have been my meat day and night, while they continually say unto me, Where is thy God?"—when that cry roll up from the deeps of the soul, the spiritual climate changes. The clouds gather in the sky, the rain of divine grace falls upon the dry and dusty field of the soul, fertility buds and blossoms on every side, the birds sing again, and life comes—sweet, precious, abundant life.

Thank God! something of that glorious experience has come into this church. In many hearts, in many homes, and to a great part of the church itself, it has been like the coming of the rainy season in the time of drought. Day after day God has poured his grace upon us, and those who had been crying for sorrow have had the new experience of crying for joy. The world outside has caught a glimpse of this new fertility, the sweet music of the melodies of our hearts has attracted their attention, and many have come to enjoy the showers of heavenly mercy and found their barrenness transformed into a garden of the Lord. I can not express to you the deep longing of my heart that the gracious influences of this divine awakening may reach every home and every heart of this church. Some of you as yet have not felt its power. You have heard about it with wondering and almost unbelieving ears, because as yet your own soul has not felt the divine touch. Do not permit these meetings to go by without sharing in this holy inspiration.

Jean Ingelow was once in the country visiting, and one evening the entire party was called out into the garden to listen to the sweet song of a nightingale. While the others were enraptured with the plaintive melody, Miss Ingelow suddenly exclaimed: "I do not hear anything at all!" Upon inquiry, they found that, being afraid of drafts, she had stuffed her ears with cotton before coming out into the night air. Alas, I fear there are some as inconsistent as that in regard to listening for the voice of God. You have closed your ears with worldliness; the jar and din of business or pleasure are so great, and so near to you, that your ears are deaf to the still small voice of the Spirit that seeks to speak to you of heavenly and divine things. Do not so rob yourself. Remember that upon you also rests the responsibility of living worthy of one who is called the brother or the sister of the Lord.

I do not doubt that I speak to some who in other places—it may be across the sea, in the old country, or in some country town or distant city—have known the forgiving love of Christ and have rejoiced in brotherly fellowship with him, but moving away from the old home, you have been caught in adverse currents, and have drifted, a sort of spiritual derelict, on the face of the waters. It is said that ships wrecked and abandoned at sea will sometimes drift thousands of miles, but if not entirely destroyed and sunk, all find their way at last into the Sargasso Sea, a portion of the North Atlantic Ocean. These modern cities are a kind of Sargasso Sea into which multitudes of church derelicts are carried, and many of them drift about, curiosity seekers, from one church to another, finding nowhere rest for their souls, until finally they are caught in some whirlpool and sink out of sight forever. Dr. Hallock tells of a little girl who had been rummaging in her mother's trunk. There she found a "church letter" which her mother had neglected to present to the church into whose neighborhood she had moved. The little explorer rushed into her mother's presence, shouting: "O mamma, I've found your religion in your trunk!" I fear there are thousands in this city to whom that incident would be an appropriate message. Surely a trunk is a dark, mothy place to keep one's religion. Wherever you may be living you should bring out your religion and put it into the spiritual exchange of some church, and let it go on its shining, helpful, living way, bearing testimony for Christ.

There is one thing we may be sure will never fail to bear rich fruit, and that is honest daily service for the Lord. The illness of Mrs. Ballington Booth called forth interest from all parts of the world. Among the many letters received by her husband was one from a man in the "condemned cell" at Sing Sing, New York. He said: "I do not belong to the Volunteer Prison League. But your wife's presence here has transformed this place in such a way that I feel good in spite of myself. When I heard she was going to die I wanted to pray, and now that the warden has told me she will get better, my heart is so full of joy that I can die in peace." What a glorious thing it is to live a life so true that Jesus is recommended by your service, and souls that are ready to give up in discouragement and despair take heart again as they see the beauty of the Christ in you!

Last Sunday I spoke to you in earnest appeal in behalf of the multitudes of young men and young women grouped all about us here, who are away from home, and need especially the Christian sympathy and fellowship which this church can give them in winning them to Christ. I was greatly impressed afterward at what Father Lewis, one of the oldest and truest pillars in our church temple, said to me in comment. He told me that nearly fifty-seven years ago, when he first came to this place from the old country, he had gone up and down these streets so lonesome and homesick that as he walked he would sob and cry as tho his heart would break out of very hunger for home and friends. Some faithful soul led young Edward Lewis to Christ, and he has been a blessing to the church and the city ever since. But I do assure you that that gold-mine is not yet worked out. There are thousands of other homesick and lonely boys and girls in this city that can be won by our Christian love and earnest devotion.

And I know I speak to many here this morning who are not Christians, who yet have a longing in your hearts to become in deed and in truth the brother or the sister of our Lord. Tho your sins pile up like mountains, over the mountains he comes with the good news of salvation. Tho your sins are blood-red like crimson or scarlet, the blood which flowed upon his cross can make them white as snow. Out of every evil association, out of the mud and mire of every wicked habit, out of the trap of every vicious and sinful way, he will lift you up on to the solid rock, up into the sunlight of loving brotherhood with himself. Do not refuse him. It is a brother's hand that is offered. It is a brother's heart that beats in sympathy with yours. It is a brother's fellowship that will make all the years to come a happy pilgrimage to the skies.

THE GREATEST THIEF IN THE WORLD IS NEGLECT.

"How shall we escape if we neglect so great salvation?"
—*Heb.* ii. 3 (Rev. Ver.).

THE greatest thief in the world is neglect. It robs more souls of heaven than anything else. The great majority of people in Christian lands who die unsaved, who go unprepared to the judgment to meet God, who are bound hand and foot by wicked habits until the last, are not lost because they did not believe God's Word. They are not lost because they are infidels. They do not fail of heaven because they were not convicted of their sin, not because they deliberately thought the matter out and came to a conclusion and said: "I will not be a Christian. I will never accept the Lord Jesus Christ as my Savior, but I will live and die as a rejecter of him." There is not one man in one hundred thousand that makes such a determination. But a great majority are unsaved because of neglect. They are waiting for some other time to come, and they put it off for lesser things until it is too late.

I read you for our Scripture lesson two of those wonderfully illuminating stories of Jesus Christ which illustrate our theme better than any merely human words.

In the first story there are ten girls who have been bidden to a wedding. They were not young ladies divided into two separate classes of wise and foolish, so that everybody knew that five of them were wise and five foolish. They were ten girls of the same social standing who moved in the same circle of acquaintance, who were accustomed to be invited to the same places, and who met together upon a plane of thorough equality. All of them, according to that Eastern custom, brought their lamps. There was a delay. The bridegroom tarried, and as the moments passed into hours they all fell asleep. It is not that five of them were awake and watchful while the other five were slumbering, but they all slept.

At last, in the midnight, the cry rang out announcing the coming of the bridegroom. At once they were aroused and full of interest and activity. With one accord each set about trimming her lamp. Then it was that five of them discovered that they had forgotten, neglected, to fill their lamps. Their oil was gone and their lamps had gone out. They tried to borrow from their more prudent associates, but they had none to spare.

Ingersoll, the infidel, flippantly points to this as a case of selfishness, but it is not so. No Christian man, however loving and good and brotherly, is able to loan the oil of salvation to his neighbor. Had it been otherwise, Ingersoll's God-fearing parents would have loaned the oil of salvation to their reckless son. Not one of us has any salvation to spare. We may cheer by our sympathy, we may encourage by a brotherly hand, we may inspire our example, we may point with loving testimony to Christ; but he only can furnish the oil of salvation. He only is great enough to save an immortal soul.

The five girls who had neglected to provide oil for their lamps hastened back into the city to buy oil and returned with rapid steps and quick-beating hearts, but the bridegroom had come in their absence and the door was closed. They cried aloud: "Open unto us! open unto us!" but the answer came: "I know you not." Their failure all turned on neglect. Perhaps they were busy, and had many cares and social engagements. Taking heed that a lamp was filled was such a little thing when so many present and noisy demands were made upon them. But on little threads like that hangs oftentimes an immortal destiny. Now there is set before you an open door, and nothing can shut it but your own neglect. Enter it while you may.

The other story is one which Christ told at a dinner, and is certainly a very heart-searching after-dinner speech; but Christ always sought to save men rather than please them. The story, as Christ tells it, is of a great feast prepared, where many invitations were sent out; and when all is ready and the hour has come for the dinner to be served there are no guests to eat it. Servants are sent to inquire the reason of the delay, and each guest sends an excuse and refuses to come. There was only one thing they united in, and that was that "They all with one consent began to make excuse." I do not suppose they had met each other and talked it over, and decided what excuse they would make. There had been no understanding among them that they would all refuse; perhaps each man that sent his excuse supposed all the rest would be there.

In two cases—of the man who had bought a farm, and the one who had bought some oxen—their business engagements cause them to neglect the feast. The man who bought the land declared that he "must" go and see it; but, as Dr. Maclaren keenly points out, this was a "must" which the man made himself. The field would not run away tho he waited until to-morrow. The bargain was finished, for he had bought it. So there was no real necessity for his going, and the next day would have done quite as well as to-day; the "must" was entirely in his own mind. Is it not so with many of you who are saying that your business relations are such that you can not now give your heart to Christ? You say glibly: "I am so pressed by necessary obligations and engagements that I really have no time to think about religion and to attend to the question of the salvation of my soul." But you are only deceiving yourself with such an answer. It is thus that the devil is cheating you. You would say at once that a man was foolish who would permit a pressing engagement connected with the investment of a thousand dollars to cause him to neglect a certain opportunity to make ten thousand dollars. How much more foolish is your course when you excuse yourself from accepting Christ's offer of salvation, which will begin here and now in forgiveness and peace, and continue in enlarged dividends of joy in a glorious immortal life.

One of the other guests in our Scripture story has another excuse of a very powerful kind. "I have married a wife," he said, "and therefore I can not come." I do not doubt there are many here who are held away from Christ because of the strong cords of the affections. Many a wife is held back because the husband, whom she tenderly loves, is not a Christian, and she fears his frown or the loss of his sympathy. I have known scores and hundreds of wives who longed to be Christians and yet neglected it because they feared to risk the sarcasm or objections of their husbands. Sometimes it is the husband, as in this case, who is held back by the unbelieving wife. Sometimes children are held back by their parents, and that seems an awful thing. I can not see how any father or mother, knowing the world and its temptations to wickedness, can go on setting an example before their children which leads them away from God and from heaven. I can not see how they can use the very cords of love for father and mother, which God has put into their young hearts, as cords to lead them away from Christ and salvation.

Now, you will notice that all these excuses are concerning things which are right in themselves. It is certainly right that a man having bought a farm should go and look after it, and carefully inquire the best way to till it and make it profitable. It is proper that a man who has bought five yoke of oxen should, as soon as convenient, yoke them up and test them. It is certainly commendable that husband or wife should give full measure of sympathy and love and presence to the home circle. But the fatal blunder and sin is that any of these things should ever be used as an excuse for neglecting the salvation of the soul. There is nothing in the Christian life which interferes with any other duties. In becoming a Christian a man does not need to sacrifice anything that he is not better without.

Some of you are in great danger of neglecting your return to God so long that you will lose out of your heart all those divine and tender memories of Christian teaching in your childhood which have so far restrained you many times from falling still deeper into sin. If a man neglects to use his best powers, he loses the ability to use them through disuse. A naturalist has just explored an island in the South Pacific, only recently discovered, and named Christmas Island. It was not thought to be inhabited by man or beast. The naturalist was, however, astounded to run across a huge bamboo house in the center of the island, and to see about it evidences of cultivation. As he appeared in the open glade an aged white man left a stockade close to the house, and, followed by his native wife and children, with a number of black servants bringing up the rear, came toward him. This modern Robinson Crusoe indicated by signs that he had forgotten his native tongue, but was vicious and warlike in his purpose, and by aid of his slaves drove the naturalist from the island. The white man gave every evidence of having relapsed completely into the barbarism of the natives. Alas, it is possible to wander away so far in sin, and give oneself up so completely to the language of the world, that the language of heaven which you learned at a prayerful mother's knee may be lost from your tongue forever!

Do not neglect the confession which you owe Christ until it is your dying confession wrung from your lips by pain and anguish. A young man, it is said, was run over by the cars last summer. On being taken to a hospital he was told that both legs must be amputated. When he asked what was likely to be the result, the surgeons were compelled to reply that the chances were largely against him, and that if he had anything he wished to say, he would better speak it at once. He was lying on the operating-table, and it was just before he was to be put under the influence of chloroform. It was a scene full of pathos. There were a number of surgeons standing around him, and several of them were not only not Christians, but inclined to be antichristian. The young man's face was contracted with pain, but he nerved himself for the declaration and said in a deep, manly voice: "My mother has long begged me to confess Christ openly; I have never done so. I regret beyond all words to express that I have neglected it so long, and I wish here and now to declare myself a soldier of the Cross, and to express my faith in

Christ and what he has wrought for us, lifting up my heart to him that he may prepare me for whatever comes." Among all those men standing about him, accustomed to scenes of pain and sorrow, there was not one whose eyes did not fill with tears at the young man's loyalty to the two greatest factors in a human life—God and mother.

An open renunciation of your sin, whatever it is, and a confession of Christ as open and brave, will certainly bring you peace and joy. Some of you have known the joy of the Lord, and have been led away by sin. You must break with that sin if you would come to Christ.

A distinguished minister from London, who was in this country last year, said that in one of his meetings there came to him a young lady who said all joy had gone out of her life four years before.

"Praise God!" he said.

"What about?" said she.

"That you know when it went; because, if you know when it went, you know how it went."

She said: "I do not think I do."

"Yes, you do; you are very definite about the time; now go back four years and tell me what happened."

She hung her head for a while, and the minister knew that something had happened. "What was it?"

She replied: "I quarreled with my oldest friend. We were both Christians and I wanted to tell her that I was wrong; but I did not, and she has gone away from the country."

"Well," the minister said, "you know all about it."

"What am I to do?" she asked.

"Write to her and tell her that you were wrong; that is what the Master wanted you to do then."

"I can not do that."

"You will never get back to the joy until you do."

Many days passed by, and there was no difference in her experience. All was darkness and despair; but one night she came to the meeting with her face all aglow with joy.

The first thing the minister said to her was: "You have sent that letter?"

"Yes," said she, and every line in her face convinced him that the gladness of salvation had returned. "I wrote it last night. I have been fighting God all these years, and this last week I have been in hell about it, and at last I said: 'O God, I can not bear this any longer, I will give in.' I wrote that letter, and sealed it, and carried it at midnight and dropped it into the letter-box, and as that letter went into the box heaven came back into my heart."

Some of you are clinging to some sin which stands between you and the heaven of joy which God longs to bring to your heart. You can never have salvation unless you give it up. Some of you are prejudiced against coming out openly to the altar and bowing down humbly before the mercy-seat; but you must be willing to do anything that is right to show forth the purpose of your heart to take Christ as your Savior. Do not let a little thing like that defraud you of heaven. You have been neglecting Christ so long, do you not owe it to him to make up for that neglect as much as you can by making your return to him as open and brave as possible?

A FRIEND WHO NEVER FAILS.

"Jesus Christ is the same yesterday and to-day, yea and forever."—*Heb.* xiii. 8 (Rev. Ver.).

CHRISTIANS who are engaged in earnest prayer and service for the salvation of their friends and neighbors ought to find great comfort in this text. Christ never failed to hear the prayer of his disciples. He was kind to them in their weakness, and in his loving conversations with them before he went away he assured them that anything they should ask of the Father in his name would be granted. He is the same loving Savior now. With all the changes that have come over the world since that day, he is not changed in the least. Eternal youth sits upon the shepherd love of Jesus Christ. You may be sure that your prayers do not fall upon ears that have grown heavy with age. We need to have this simple, childlike faith in Christ, not only for the comfort of our own hearts, but that we may thus claim the divine promise for others.

A man had been bringing his brother to church for some time, hoping that he would be converted, and one evening, to the great joy of his heart, his brother made an open confession of Christ and was most happily saved. After the service was over his pastor said to him, "I suppose you were surprised to see him converted."

"I should have been very much surprised if he had not been," was the answer.

"But why, my dear brother?" said the minister.

"Because," said he, "I asked the Lord to convert him, and I kept on praying that he might be converted; and I should have been very much surprised if he had not been."

That is what I mean by childlike faith that rests upon the promises of God and expects that prayer will be answered.

We may be sure that the Christ who when he was here on earth brought about great results by means of the little things that his friends offered him, is still the same loving and powerful friend, who will multiply every honest service we do for him. He who did not discard or treat with contempt the little lad's five loaves and two fishes, but gave his blessing to them and multiplied them to feed the multitude, will not scorn your service, tho it may seem to you as only a cup of cold water. If your heart's love go with your effort, and it is your best, Christ will take it and multiply it, and cause it to do immeasurable good in the salvation of souls.

A young telegraph-boy had been for a long time convicted of sin. He was constantly burdened with the consciousness that he had done wrong, and that in some way he needed divine help, but he was befogged and in the dark. He was almost discouraged; religion seemed to him something vague and unreal, and he was about to give up in despair of there being for him such a thing as Christian joy. But as he sat at his telegraph instrument one day, a man came in and, asking for a blank, wrote out a despatch and handed it to him. As he took the telegram in his hand to transmit it, it was with great surprise that he spelled out these words: "Behold the Lamb of God, which taketh away the sin of the world." A Christian man who was out for a holiday had received that morning a letter from a friend who was in great trouble of soul, and tho he had answered the letter, it occurred to him that a telegram would reach him quicker, and might give him the help he needed. His loving thought saved two souls—not only the man at the end of the line, but the young telegrapher who transmitted it. It was God's message to him. He saw that he had been casting about after all sorts of things when the one thing in the world that he needed was to look to Christ, and as his fingers touched the keys to send the message over the wire, the Holy Spirit applied the words to his own heart, and he beheld the Lamb of God bearing not only the sins of the world, but his own sins.

Mr. Spurgeon tells how Dr. Valpy wrote four simple lines as his confession of faith:

> "In peace let me resign my breath,
>   And thy salvation see;
> My sins deserve eternal death,
>   But Jesus died for me."

Valpy soon died, but he had given the lines to Dr. Marsh, the rector at Beckenham, who put them over his study mantel-shelf. The Earl of Roden came in and read them. "Will you give me a copy of those lines?" inquired the good Earl. "I shall be glad to," said Dr. Marsh, and he copied them. Lord Roden took them home, and put them over *his* mantel-shelf. General Taylor, a Waterloo hero, came into the room, and noticed them. He read them over and over again, while staying with Earl Roden, till his Lordship remarked, "I say, friend Taylor, I should think you might know those lines by heart." He answered, with deep emotion: "I do know them by heart; indeed, my very heart has grasped their meaning." The great soldier was brought to Christ by that humble rime. General Taylor in turn copied the lines, and handed them to an officer in the army who was going out to the Crimean war. Afterward he came home to die. Dr. Marsh went to see him, and the dying soldier said: "Good sir, do you know this verse which General Taylor gave to me? It brought me to my Savior, and I die in peace." To Dr. Marsh's surprise he repeated the lines:

> "In peace let me resign my breath,
> And thy salvation see;
> My sins deserve eternal death,
> But Jesus died for me."

Think how God blessed the work of that good man, and sent the four lines which he had written in grateful love from one heart to another, carrying salvation with them everywhere. It is the same Jesus who is our Savior and our Friend, and he loves us just as much as he did Dr. Valpy, or any of the early disciples, and with the tenderest love he receives our service and will bless it to the salvation of souls.

This is also a blessed Scripture for you who are not Christians. He is the very same Jesus that he was when on earth, and we know that then he was always willing to save. "Come unto me, all ye that labor and are heavy laden," was the cry of Jesus when he was here on earth, going about doing good, and he is still calling the weary and the heavy laden to come to him that they may find rest unto their souls. When Christ was here he was the most pitiful man that ever lived toward those whose sins had brought them into the deepest sorrow, and had left them friendless and discouraged. No influence of a mob could frighten him into cursing the poor woman who had been taken in adultery; neither would he, in order to court the favor of the rich and powerful, turn a cold look or a forbidding gesture to the publicans and sinners who gathered to hear him. He is the same Jesus to-day, his heart is as full of pity and sympathy for sinners as it was then, and he is still saying to broken, downcast hearts, "Neither do I condemn thee: go, and sin no more." He is just as ready to say to you now, as he ever was to anybody, "Thy sins, which are many, are forgiven thee."

When Christ was here, he was one of the easiest of men to get acquainted with. Nobody needed to have a titled friend or a rich neighbor to introduce him to Jesus. The letter of introduction that was most sure to get his immediate and unconditional love and friendship was to have blind eyes, or deaf ears, or the scales of leprosy that made every one else afraid; or to be possessed with devils so that you were shunned by your neighbors. If you were in need of a friend, and your heart was hungry for somebody to love you and say cheering words to you, heal you of your sickness, or set you free from a cruel bondage, you were sure of immediate attention and kindly treatment at the hands of Jesus Christ. Anybody could approach him; even the poor leper that had to cry "unclean, unclean" to everybody else, could draw near to Christ without a frown. Thank God! he is still the same approachable, loving Savior; he has not become conservative or aristocratic or reserved and distant in his habits since he ascended on high. Ah! no, his very business in heaven keeps him in touch with us, for he is at the right hand of God making intercessions for us. The Christ who calmed the stormy waves at a word; who touched the leper and said: "I will; be thou clean"; he who called to Lazarus, "Come forth!" and the dead man stood living again, is the very same Jesus still, ready to heal and quicken into life. He has lost none of his sympathy or his power. "He is able also to save them to the uttermost that come unto God by him, seeing he ever liveth to make intercession for them."

When Christ was here in his earthly ministry, one of the most astonishing things about him was the way he trusted people. He had that divine insight into the human heart that could see the goodness hidden under all the sin, and by his confidence he saved the souls of those whom others thought to be untrustworthy. It is often a man's salvation to have somebody trust him. There is an interesting incident told of the Duke of York, the heir to the English crown. While yet Prince George, he was serving on the West Indian squadron, and was put in command of the steamship *Thrush*. The following day a sailor in irons was brought on board the vessel to be transported to another part of the station. The prisoner was but a lad of the same age as the young commander, and there was something in his face and bearing, reckless tho he was, that showed that he was not wholly bad. Prince George watched him keenly during the short voyage, and after he had delivered him up for punishment, made a note of the time when his imprisonment would be over. When the day came he applied to the admiral to have the man transferred to the *Thrush*. The admiral remonstrated, urging that it was not the prisoner's first offense, that he had been drunken and disorderly for two years. "Let me try what I can do," said the prince. The admiral reluctantly consented, and when the prisoner came on board the *Thrush* he was brought before the young captain. When they were alone together, the boy **whom fortune had made a prince said to the boy** whose surroundings had helped to make him an outcast: "You have been transferred to my ship. I believe there is some good in you, and I wish to give you a chance for your life. You are given a clean sheet for your record. The first-class men go ashore to-day on special leave. Go with them. You have had no leave for a year. I exact no promise of good behavior from you, and trust wholly to your honor. I hope you will not disappoint me. Here is a sovereign. You know what you ought and ought not to do as well as I know, and if you offend again you must go back to the class from which I now remove you. Your future is in your own hands." The man proved worthy of the trust. He has been so honest and efficient a sailor that he has now been promoted to be an officer. Should Prince George, now Duke, ever become king, he will have no more loyal, faithful subject than the man whom he saved from moral ruin.

But that is only a faint type of the way Jesus Christ, our Savior, is ready to treat you. He will not only forgive you your past sins and give you a clean record, but he will give you a clean heart, and will himself dwell in your heart, a sacred guest, strengthening there every good impulse, every noble ambition, and giving you his own strong arm to lean upon, so that day by day you shall have his friendship to cheer and inspire you.

THE SWORD THAT CUTS BOTH WAYS.

"For the word of God is living, and active, and sharper than any two-edged sword."—*Heb.* iv. 12 (Rev. Ver.).

THE illustrations that are used to describe the Word of God throughout the Bible suggest its energy and power. It is compared in the Psalms to a lamp, a light to guide the feet. Light is positive; darkness is negative. Light dispels darkness. The rays of the sun flash from world to world across millions of miles of space in time measured by seconds, and that is only a faint type of the flashing of spiritual light. Again, the Word of God is compared to a hammer to break the rock in pieces, so that no opposition can withstand it. In Jeremiah it is said, "Is not my word like as a fire? saith the Lord." Nothing is more active, more vital with life, than fire. It is at once heat and light. It melts and consumes. It either warms into life, or it annihilates. It is also compared to a seed, an incorruptible seed which supplies the moral harvests of the world. A seed is full of life; one can easily imagine a giant oak-tree, whose shadows fall for a hundred feet, bound up in an acorn. One looks at the heap of wheat on the granary floor and beholds a wide-reaching field of waving grain shimmering in the sun. A seed is the most powerful thing in nature. No giant that ever lived could lift such loads as a seed that a sparrow could swallow. Wooed by the sunshine and the shower, nerved by the omnipotent life which God has given it, it can tear a stone wall to pieces, lift a weight of many tons, and push anything aside which stands between it and the light.

We are therefore not surprised to find the Word of God compared in this text to a sword—and not only to a sword, but one sharper than "any two-edged sword." There have been many sharp two-edged swords in the earth, subjected, like the far-famed Damascus blades, to the most ingenious temperings of the swordmaker's art; but Paul declares that the Word of God is sharper than any of them. Shakespeare must have had this text in his mind where he speaks of "the mind's eye" which flashes through all the sensations and actions of the soul like lightning, and lays bare to a man's consciousness all that God has detected within him. There is life in the Word of God. It is living and active to awaken the slumberer, to cut deep beneath the surface and make man know himself.

Dr. Thomas Armitage says that certain historic things need corroborating evidence outside of themselves, but some things are self-evident. The sun tells of its own light, and you can not well prove it; your pulse tells of your own life, and you can not demonstrate it by reasoning. So the sharp, keen sword of the Word of God shows a man's inner heart to himself. Jesus Christ talked only for a little while with the woman at the well of Samaria, but his conversation served to open every dark corner of her heart and let the light in upon every sin; and wicked deeds that she had forgotten came out from their moldy resting-places where they had been slumbering for years and shook themselves into horrid life again. So deeply and keenly did the word from Christ cleave into the soul of that woman that it opened to her her whole history at one gash, and when she went into the town to tell her acquaintances about it she declared he must indeed be the Messiah, for, says she, "He told me all things that ever I did."

God's Word has not lost its power to cut sharp between the lower and the higher life, or to discern the secret things of the heart. It is the heart that must be opened to the light if we are to be saved, for it is the heart that has gone astray. It is in the heart that evil imaginations are born, and where unholy thoughts are hatched out into wicked plans and purposes. The wise man of old did well to urge the guarding of the heart with all diligence, declaring that out of it are the issues of life. Christ says that out of the heart proceed evil thoughts, which manifest themselves in every wicked way. It is the infinite love of God that leads him to use the sharp sword of his Word in opening up to our gaze the wickedness of our hearts. It has been well said that perhaps no sight on earth is so painful as that of a skilful surgeon whose mind is keyed to the highest tension, till his nerve is as steady as the magnetic needle, and his judgment as cool as the north star to which it points, and in this frame of mind is operating upon a suffering patient. It appears to an unthinking mind like the height of cold-blooded heartlessness for him to be able to grasp the knife so firmly and, without a twinge or wince, almost at one stroke, sever the joint at the socket, or lay bare the bone and pierce to the marrow. Yet perhaps there is no more benevolent deed performed on earth than that of the skilful surgeon who, when it is necessary, does not hesitate to cut off the right hand, or pluck out the right eye, or to remove the deadly tumor. And the more thoroughly self-possessed, accurate, and cool the act on his part, the better for the sufferer, the lighter his torture, and the surer his cure. When gangrene threatens a wound, it is better that a part of the body should be promptly removed than that the whole body should perish. The skilful surgeon does not give pain for his own pleasure, but for the profit and salvation of his patient. Neither does God pierce our hearts with the sharp two-edged sword of his Word until strong men cry out in agony because of their sin, but that we may be aroused to our peril, that our souls may be saved. See Peter at Pentecost tracing the coming of Jesus Christ through the prophecies, until he reaches the birth of Jesus, then following him on through his ministry, showing that all the prophecies concerning the Messiah were fulfilled in Jesus, and that he indeed was the Savior for whom they had been looking. Then with flashing eyes he turns upon them, and the Holy Spirit gives power to the Word as he charges it straight home to the men standing before him, and declares that they themselves had taken Christ with cruel hands and murdered him on the cross, and that God had raised him from the dead. In Peter's hand the sharp sword of God's Word pierced these men to their hearts, and instead of being angry with the messenger, or seeking to harm him for his faithfulness, the sword of God so showed them their own wickedness that they cried aloud: "Men and brethren, what shall we do?" But God had not been piercing their hearts with a sword simply to torment them. He did it to show them the deadly gangrene of sin in their hearts, so that they might be healed and saved, and that very day three thousand of those haters of Jesus Christ were happily converted and added to the infant church.

God's Word has not lost its power. We have seen men and women pierced to the heart by the simple Word of God, and beheld them turning to Christ and finding in him the joy of salvation. God's Word is cutting like a sword in some of your consciences now. Some of you were here last evening, when so many were convicted, and the two-edged sword of the Spirit thrust through all the armor of your self-complacency, and cut deep down into your heart, and made you confess to your inner self that you were a poor wretched sinner. But startled as you were, and condemned as you felt, you tried to hush your conscience, and thrust your sins back into the darkness. All night, and all day long, you have been trying to patch up your armor so that you might parry or turn aside the sharp thrusts of God's Word. But how unwise it is thus to attempt to blind yourself to your own condition. Would any wise man desire to be in ignorance of the deadly cancer that every day was getting a stronger hold on the vital forces of his life? Would he not rather welcome you will probably remember how he describes an incident in the imprisonment of Montigny. For a long time he had been shut up in the castle at Segovia. He was in despair and waited hopelessly for death. But one day there passed through the streets of the little town a band of Flemish pilgrims chanting, as was the custom in those times, a low, monotonous song. Theirs was a strange tongue, and they were not understood by those about them. But the prisoner, as he listened, found they were singing the language of his own country, and singing for him. And so their real message, all unsuspected by the passing crowds, they sang to him,—of hope, and a way of escape. Some of you, it may be, are in discouragement and despair as the Word of God shows you the sinfulness of your own heart. You feel as if you were imprisoned by wicked habits, and as tho the key were held by your enemy. If such is your case, I come to you as a messenger of God's love to stand beneath your prison window and sing the song of redeeming mercy. Whoever else passes on without heeding it, you who know your sin and your bondage ought to listen; for I sing you a song of liberty, of sunny skies, of peace, and God. I sing you the song of him who has declared: "Him that cometh to me I will in no wise cast out," and who is able to save "unto the uttermost." For this sword of God is a two-edged sword—the edge that cuts sharp and keen into your consciences, revealing your sins, is not keener than the edge of love that seeks to save you.

The warden of an Eastern state prison tells this wonderful story of the power of love: He was passing out of the prison yard one bitterly cold Christmas morning. Just outside the gate, and crouching close to the high stone wall, he saw a thinly clad little girl of about twelve years, her face and hands blue with cold. She put out one of her thin hands to detain him as he passed.

"If you please, sir," she said, and stopped, fingering nervously at the fringe of her old shawl, and timidly glancing down.

"What is it?" he asked.

"If you please, sir, I'd like to know if I can go inside and see my—my father. He's in there, and I've brung him something for Christmas. It ain't much, and I didn't spose you'd mind any if he had it. His name is John ——."

He recognized the name as that of a life convict—a man notoriously bad. He went back into the prison grounds, the child following him eagerly. Going to his office, the warden sent for the convict. He came, sullen and dejected; in his face was the look of utter hopelessness which the faces of the life prisoners so often wear. The child sprang you will probably remember how he describes an incident in the imprisonment of Montigny. For a long time he had been shut up in the castle at Segovia. He was in despair and waited hopelessly for death. But one day there passed through the streets of the little town a band of Flemish pilgrims chanting, as was the custom in those times, a low, monotonous song. Theirs was a strange tongue, and they were not understood by those about them. But the prisoner, as he listened, found they were singing the language of his own country, and singing for him. And so their real message, all unsuspected by the passing crowds, they sang to him,—of hope, and a way of escape. Some of you, it may be, are in discouragement and despair as the Word of God shows you the sinfulness of your own heart. You feel as if you were imprisoned by wicked habits, and as tho the key were held by your enemy. If such is your case, I come to you as a messenger of God's love to stand beneath your prison window and sing the song of redeeming mercy. Whoever else passes on without heeding it, you who know your sin and your bondage ought to listen; for I sing you a song of liberty, of sunny skies, of peace, and God. I sing you the song of him who has declared: "Him that cometh to me I will in no wise cast out," and who is able to save "unto the uttermost." For this sword of God is a two-edged sword—the edge that cuts sharp and keen into your consciences, revealing your sins, is not keener than the edge of love that seeks to save you.

The warden of an Eastern state prison tells this wonderful story of the power of love: He was passing out of the prison yard one bitterly cold Christmas morning. Just outside the gate, and crouching close to the high stone wall, he saw a thinly clad little girl of about twelve years, her face and hands blue with cold. She put out one of her thin hands to detain him as he passed.

"If you please, sir," she said, and stopped, fingering nervously at the fringe of her old shawl, and timidly glancing down.

"What is it?" he asked.

"If you please, sir, I'd like to know if I can go inside and see my—my father. He's in there, and I've brung him something for Christmas. It ain't much, and I didn't spose you'd mind any if he had it. His name is John ——."

He recognized the name as that of a life convict —a man notoriously bad. He went back into the prison grounds, the child following him eagerly. Going to his office, the warden sent for the convict. He came, sullen and dejected; in his face was the look of utter hopelessness which the faces of the life prisoners so often wear. The child sprang forward to meet him, the hot tears streaming over her white face. He stepped back, sullen and seemingly angry. No word of welcome came from his lips for the ragged, trembling little creature who stood crying before him, with something clasped in her hands.

"I—I—came to say, 'Merry Christmas,' father," she faltered. "I—I—thought maybe you'd be glad to see me. Ain't you any glad, father?"

"Christmas!" What would that man not have given for freedom of body and soul! His head drooped. The hard look was going out of his face, his eyes were moistening.

His little girl went on, trembling, and tearfully: "I—I—brung you something, father. It was all I could think of, and all I could get. I live at the poor-house now."

Her trembling fingers began unwrapping the bit of soft white paper in her hand, and she held out a short, shining curl of yellow hair, carefully tied with a bit of old ribbon. "I wouldn't give this to anybody on earth but you, father. You used to truly, really love little Johnny. Mother said you did—and so——"

The man fell on his knees with both hands clasped over his face. "I did love him," he said, hoarsely. "I love him still; bad as I am, I love him still."

"I know it," said the child, going closer, "and I knowed you'd like this, now that Johnny's dead."

"Dead! dead!" wailed the broken-hearted man, rocking to and fro still on his knees with his hands over his face. "My little boy?"

"Yes," said the child, "he died in the poorhouse only last week, and there's no one left but me now. But I ain't going to forget you, father. I'm going to stick right by you, 'spite of what folks say, and some day maybe I can get you out of here. I'm going to try. I don't never forget that you are my father, and so——"

But sin and hate and anger and sullenness were no match for a love like that, and the man threw out his arms and gathered the little one to his breast and kissed her again and again as tho his lips were hungry for love. All the sullenness of his heart gave way, and with it seemed to go the hopelessness and the awful bitterness, and the two, clasped in each other's arms, wept and prayed together. When they separated an hour later there were tears on both faces, but love smiled back through the tears from the face of the wicked man as surely as from the face of the little girl.

If the love of a little child could do that, what shall not the all-encompassing love of Jesus Christ perform? He not only came down from heaven to suffer shame and poverty and ignominy and death for you, but through all the years of your wandering has watched over you with patient love, even when you have slighted him and grieved his tender heart and rejected his offers of mercy. Still he comes back to you again and again, and says with yearning love: "I haven't forgotten you, no matter who else has forgotten you, nor how your sin has disgraced you. I am still seeking to save you."

Will you not cry out in the language of the old hymn?—

> "Just as I am—thy love unknown
> Hath broken every barrier down;
> Now, to be thine, yea, thine alone,
> O Lamb of God, I come! I come!"

THROWING THE SOUL'S PURSUERS OFF THE SCENT.

"The sin which doth so easily beset us."—*Heb.* xii. 1 (Rev. Ver.).

I NEVER think of this Scripture but there comes back to my memory an experience of the War of the Rebellion which a man once related to me. He was a prisoner in a Southern prison, and managed, with some others, to escape, and after almost intolerable hardship they reached the North and their homes. They were pursued by bloodhounds, and he said that no other trouble or threat of trouble that had come to him in the course of an eventful life ever made such a horrid sensation in his breast as the baying of those bloodhounds. At last they were chased so hotly that they saw they must soon be overtaken and probably fearfully mangled by the cruel beasts unless they could in some way throw their pursuers off the scent. Suddenly they came on a lagoon, or dead slough, in the edge of a swamp. The water was filthy, but into it they went, wading where they could, sometimes being compelled to swim, but not daring to leave the stagnant stream, where sometimes deadly moccasin snakes writhed near them. They pushed on, keeping as closely under cover as possible, and remained in this water for hours, until they had completely thrown off the bloodhounds that had been following them.

It seems to me a man's besetting sin is like that. There never was a bloodhound so vicious or cruel as a besetting sin that has seized hold of the natural weakness of a man's soul and pursues him like a Nemesis when he endeavors to throw off the bondage of evil and enter upon a pure and good life. Across all the fair promise of the man's new hope and purpose will come the deep baying of the bloodhounds of some old appetite that has terrorized him because it has so often thwarted his desire to live worthy of his manhood.

Years ago I had a friend with as many good qualities as almost any man I have ever known—honest, genuine, true-hearted, in every way a man to admire and respect, a man with a wide circle of influential friends and comrades, and who, most of the time, could have been pointed out by every fond mother as a model of the courteous, refined, honorable gentleman. But he had his besetting sin, and tho sometimes he fought it off for six months at a time, after about so long the blood-curdling notes of his bloodhound would ring in his ears. His sin took the form of appetite for strong drink. His pride would not let him go to the saloon, but when he had come to the end of his strength he would take the liquor home with him, and there, day after day and night after night, he would fill himself with the accursed poison. After two or three weeks he would reach the point where a physician must come in to save his life, and he would slowly beat his way back again to manly strength. No one who does not know what struggles such men make can for a moment conceive of the shame and sorrow, the remorse and the despair, which he suffered in those days when he trembled back into himself. He was not a Christian, of course. But in every struggle the man could possibly make, he wrestled for victory as I have never seen any other man; yet that deadly sin was ever on his track. Finally, I was able, by the grace of God, to persuade him to take Jesus Christ at his word, as simply as would a little child, and to trust him who has declared his willingness and power to set us free. From that day he has had liberty. The blood of Jesus Christ so washed away the sin of his heart that even that devil's bloodhound of appetite was thrown off the scent, and in the years that have passed since then he has grown increasingly stronger. Today he is a joyous and useful Christian, whose strong arm, generous hand, and courageous heart are among the chief pillars of support of every good movement in his church and community.

I do not know what your besetting sin is, but as I have been speaking some of you have been keenly conscious of the sin that pursues you with such fiendish malignity. You, too, have tried in your own strength to escape from its pursuit. You have forsworn it again and again, and there have been times when you had hope. It may be you have been so taken up with other things that for a space you have escaped its deadly threat; but at an hour when you thought yourself safest, your besetting sin has thrust its villainous head out from under the forest of life and chilled your blood with its horrid cry of pursuit. You can not overcome it in your own strength. The reason is that deep down in your heart there is the citadel of sin and rebellion against God. Every day that you refuse to give Christ the open affection and love of your heart, the frank and avowed testimony of your daily service, you are sinning against him who is your rightful Master and Lord.

This sin is weakening your will. It is paralyzing your power of decision, and rendering you helpless in your attempt to escape from "the sin which doth so easily beset." Some of you with gray hairs coming on your head are not able yet to decide. The fact is, that sin has undermined your power of will. You have seen a man with shaking palsy—his brain gives the order to stretch forth his hand and take a glass of water from the table, but he no longer has physical ability to carry out the command of the brain, or, rather, the brain has lost its perfect control of nerve and muscle, and the hand goes trembling and shaking on its mission, as if undecided. My heart has been saddened beyond description to see some who are past middle life and who for many years have known the vile and dangerous character of sin, and now really long to come to Christ, whose power to will to choose Christ seems to be paralyzed. Their moral nature has become wavering, trembling, and uncertain. Day after day, tho convicted by the Spirit of God, they are unable to say to God, "I will," while they dare not say, "I will not"; and thus halting between two opinions they suffer untold sorrow and agony, but seem not to have the power to take the cup of happiness which Christ offers them. I beg of you, young men and young women, do not go on in your sins until you shall become like that; but choose Christ, and act upon your choice here and now.

In order to have salvation, sin must be given up. But you are infinitely better off with it given up. I doubt not you have all heard of Uncle John

Vassar. He became one of the most remarkable soul-winners of his time. He was converted when he was about twenty-five years of age, being then at work in his uncle's brewery in Poughkeepsie. There was not so much said about temperance in those days, and a great many people thought that a man could make beer and still be a Christian. After he was converted, John Vassar made a little rack above the vat where he was at work in the brewery, on which he kept his Bible. He wanted to have his Bible there so he could study it. But soon there came an explosion. You may be sure there will always be an explosion when you take the Word of God where there is any kind of intoxicating liquor. This explosion blew John Vassar clear out of the brewery, and he never went back. His wealthy uncle offered to raise his wages, and finally offered to take him into partnership, but John said: "No, I will have nothing to do with this accursed thing." God wonderfully blessed him, and gave him thousands of jewels for the Master's crown. Who would not rather be in heaven, as Uncle John Vassar is to-day, enjoying the society of the thousands of men and women whom he led to Christ, than, after leading others astray all his life, to be in hell, having left the largest brewery on the Hudson River behind him to do the devil's work in the years to come?

But the point I wanted to impress is, that when John Vassar made up his mind that he was to be a Christian, and go nowhere except where his Bible could go, all manner of sin and himself had to part fellowship. If you desire to get rid of your besetting sin you must do away with all sin; for all sin is akin, and it is not possible to cherish rebellion in your heart against God, and reject Christ as your Savior, and at the same time escape that one besetting sin of which you are ashamed.

Many of you would come to Christ at once if it were not that some secret sins are holding you back, causing you to reject Christ's offer of salvation. With some of you the besetting sin is that of the young man that came to Christ, whose outward life was so correct and admirable that Jesus, looking upon him, loved him. Yet he went away with a cloud on his brow and sorrow in his heart, because of his secret devotion to the things of the world. Some of you are staying away because at the heart, tho you would not admit it, you are cowardly. You are afraid of being laughed at and twitted by some of your associates, and you are in sad danger of being laughed out of your soul. What a pitiable thing it would be to miss heaven and eternal life for fear of somebody's silly sneer! Another is being held back because of a secret sin of impurity. A guilty passion has led you astray, and holds you in its deadly grip. To be a Christian means to break with that. In God's name do not let your lowest nature defeat your highest. Do not let the animal strangle to death the angel within you! Here is another whose sin is simply putting off the confession of Jesus, but he has put it off so long that a deadly lethargy holds him to his seat. Oh, my friends, whatever it is that holds you back, count up all the cost and choose Christ now! Break away from every sinful appetite and passion, from every unholy purpose, and come to Jesus, who is able to transform your heart and character into his own noble image!

But the devil whispers to some of you: "You can not come. You have sinned against the Lord so long, and so grieved the Holy Spirit, that you have no right to come." Ah! but you have a right to come since he asks you. The foreman in a large machine factory was under conviction of sin and was greatly troubled, but the devil made him believe that he had been a sinner so long that he had no right to come to Christ. The owner of the factory, who was a good Christian man, found out the situation, and sent around to the works a card on which he had written, "Come to my house immediately after work." When the foreman appeared at his employer's door, the employer came out and said roughly: "What do you want, John, troubling me at this time? Work is done for to-day. What right have you here?"

"Sir," said he, greatly surprised at his master's conduct, "I had a card from you saying that I was to come after work."

"Do you mean to say that merely because you had a card from me you are to come up to my house, and call me out after business hours?"

"Well, sir," replied the foreman, "I do not understand you, but it seems to me that, as you sent for me, I had a right to come."

"Come in, John," said his employer. "I have another message that I want to read to you." And he took down the Bible and read, "Come unto me, all ye that labor and are heavy laden, and I will give you rest." "Do you think after such a message from Christ that you can be wrong in going to him?"

The foreman saw the point at once, and from that hour entered into the joys of salvation. Follow his example now!

DRIFTING OUT OF THE TRACK OF THE HOME SHIPS.

"Therefore we ought to give the more earnest heed to the things that were heard, lest haply we drift away from them."—*Heb.* ii. 1 (Rev. Ver.).

THERE is an unmarked track across the seas—that is, it is unmarked except on the ocean charts—along which the great ocean steamers make their journey from land to land. If a shipwreck occurs, or the captain in any way loses control of his vessel, his greatest anxiety is not to drift out of the track of ships that might be able to give him help, and either tow his vessel homeward or at least take on board his passengers and crew. To drift out of the track of the home ships is to drift into the greatest peril of irretrievable disaster.

Two years ago the bark *Celadon* was on her voyage from Australia to Honolulu, and was not far from Hawaii, when a gale blew her off and cast her upon a sunken reef. The captain and crew, fifteen men all told, were compelled to take to the two small boats. They succeeded in getting off only a few cans of provisions, a bag or two of sea biscuit, and a keg of water, before the ship went to pieces. With this food they hoped to make their way to some island.

But they found no land, and their supplies rapidly became exhausted. They were under the equator, and all day the sun beat down upon them mercilessly. For a time water was served out to the men by the spoonful, at the rate of eight spoonfuls a day to each. The heat increased their thirst, but the ration of water had to be reduced. At last a shower fell. Each boat was provided with a sail, and the men wrung out the sails and added a few drops of water to their scanty store. They were slowly dying of hunger and thirst.

Finally the captain died, and they took the only sack which they had brought with them, and, putting the body in it, committed it to the waves; the men with thick utterance and wailing voices joining in the service for the dead.

On the twenty-third day of their drifting, every scrap of their food was gone. They had a little water left.

On the thirtieth day the mate lay down in the bottom of the boat, prepared to go to sleep. "If you get sight of land inside of five hours," he said, "wake me up; if not, let me stay asleep for good and all."

All at once one of the men called out, "I see land!"

Some thought him crazy, but all pulled with their waning strength in the direction he pointed out. Sure enough, a little wooded coral reef came into view. They let the waves, which were running rather high, cast them on the reef.

Two natives, Fijians, soon came running down, with hatchets and long knives, as if to put the intruders to death; but seeing their pitiful condition, they went from threats to kindness. They helped them to land, and prepared food for them.

One man was so near gone that he died on reaching the land. The other thirteen soon revived under the kind treatment of the two natives. They found that they were on an isle called Sophie Island, and that only two families of natives lived there; furthermore, that it was entirely out of the track of ships, that no vessel ever came to this little isle, and that it was so far from all other land as to make hopeless the attempt to reach any port.

So these men settled down to a half-savage existence, like thirteen Robinson Crusoes, hoping against hope for deliverance. They built a hut among the coconut-trees, and caught turtles and fish, and these with the coconuts served to keep them alive. But as the months went by their homesickness grew intense. They were Norwegians, and most of them had families in faraway Norway; they guessed at the date of Christmas, and tried to have a little celebration of the holy festival, but it ended in bitter tears of awful loneliness. From the very first day of their landing they had kept a signal of distress flying from the highest point on the island, and kept one of their number continually on guard watching for a sail. Sometimes they saw a speck in the distance, and hope would flutter at their hearts, only to give way to growing despair as the ship faded out in the distance without taking notice of their signal.

But last July a ship did come. It seemed to observe their signal, and three of the men threw themselves into a canoe and paddled off to the visitor. It proved to be the drill-ship *Clyde*, of the British navy. The captain took the castaways on board, and by way of Australia and London they reached home, to the joy of their loved ones, who had given them up for dead.

Our text suggests a similar danger which threatens every man or woman who drifts upon the sea of life without definitely choosing the heavenly port. Dr. Marcus Dods declares that it is mainly by drifting, by letting things slide, by trusting to luck or to nature, that people come to grief. All our observation shows us that it is not enough to be simply in a state of moral indifference; it is not enough not to choose evil. The only safety lies in positively and strongly choosing the good, and steering that way with all the force we have. The man who becomes a drunkard did not determine to be a drunkard, he only drifted; he did not choose a clean, sober manhood, and steer toward that with all the force of his soul. An energetic and positive choice necessarily lies at the root of all moral growth. One of the great curses of humanity is drifting. The great men and women who achieve mighty deeds, and whose influence is uplifting and blessed, are never people who drift about and trust to luck or chance. They are people who choose their course, and having made their decision stand by it with a tenacity stronger than life itself.

I beg of you, if you are drifting away from God, drifting away from the Bible, drifting away from habits of prayer, that you will take notice that you are drifting out of the track of the home ships that might give you help in the salvation of your soul. If some of you were to carefully think it over, I am sure you would be astonished to notice how far you have drifted away from heavenly and divine things since your childhood. There was a time when it would have been impossible for you to go to sleep at night without conscientiously reviewing your conduct during the day, and earnestly and tenderly praying to God to forgive anything that was wrong in it, and committing all that you had to his care. There was a time when sleep would never have come to your eyelids without that; but how far some of you have drifted! How long has it been since you really prayed? Or it may be that still the power of habit causes you to say a line or two of prayer that you learned at your mother's knee, but how long since, with conscious earnestness, you lifted your heart to God in thanksgiving or in a plea for forgiveness? I fear some of you would be ashamed to acknowledge how utterly prayerless your life has come to be. You eat your food, you lie down at night and fall asleep, you rise up in the morning and go about your work, with no word of thanksgiving or prayer, as tho there were no God, as tho you had no soul to save, as tho there were no heaven to win or hell to shun. Alas! how far you have drifted from the track of Mercy's ships that are likely to carry a soul to heaven!

Some of you recall, while I speak in this vein, the Christian atmosphere of that old home where you grew up, an atmosphere made fragrant with the reading of the Bible and sweet songs of love and praise to Christ. Perhaps your mother, like mine, loved to sing the old hymns, and childhood as you look back on it seems full of Christian music. Perhaps the home is broken up now and the family scattered, and you have no hope of ever seeing that family group again unless perchance you catch the ship of *Mercy* for heaven, and meet them all before the throne of God. Perhaps the mother herself has ceased to sing on earth and has gone up to the heavenly choir.

"Hushed are those lips, their earthly song is ended;
 The singer sleeps at last;
While I sit gazing at her armchair, vacant,
 And think of days long past.

"The room still echoes with the old-time music,
 As, singing, soft and low,
Those grand, sweet hymns, the Christian's consolation,
 She rocks her to and fro.

"Some that can stir the heart like shouts of triumph,
 Or loud-toned trumpet's call,
Bidding the people prostrate fall before him,
 'And crown him—Lord of all.'

"And tender notes, filled with melodious rapture,
 That leaned upon his word,
Rose in those strains of solemn, deep affection,
 'I love thy kingdom, Lord.'

"Safe hidden in the wondrous 'Rock of Ages,'
 She bade farewell to fear;
Sure that her Lord would always gently lead her,
 She read her 'title clear.'

"Joyful she saw 'from Greenland's icy mountains'
  The gospel flag unfurled ;
 And knew by faith 'the morning light was breaking'
  Over a sinful world.

"'There is a fountain,' how the tones triumphant
  Rose in victorious strains,
 'Filled with that precious blood, for all the ransomed,
  Drawn from Immanuel's veins.'

"In minor tones she sang of God's great judgments ;
  Broad was the sinner's road,
 Where thousands walked, forgetful of his mercy,
  To death's dark, dread abode.

"Then, changing to a mood more sweet and tender,
  The notes would softer be,
 Speaking with joy of his great loving kindness
  Unchanging, sure, and free.

"Sometimes, when hope was faint and storm-clouds
    gathered,
  And darkened seemed the day,
 Rose like a dirge, 'I would not live here alway,
  I ask thee not to stay.'

"Then, filled with faith's diviner inspiration,
  'O rise, my soul,' she cries,
 'Stretch out thy wings and trace thy better portion,
  Press onward to the prize.'

"Dear saint, in heavenly mansions long since folded,
  Safe in God's fostering love,
 She joins with rapture in the blissful chorus
  Of those bright choirs above.

> "There, where no tears are known, no pain or sorrow,
>   Safe beyond Jordan's roll,
> She lives forever with her blessed Jesus,
>   'The lover of her soul.'"

I am sure that some of you feel with sadness and with a deep conviction of sin that you have drifted far from the holy atmosphere that prompted your mother's songs, or that filled with simple confidence and trust your childhood's prayers. And the longer you continue to drift the farther you are going away from God and heaven. To-night we come to you with the life-boat, longing to have the joy of bringing you back from your wandering, back to the home port of prayer and thanksgiving and fellowship with God.

Tho some of you have not found the rags of the prodigal, or the hunger of the starving sailors; tho it may be that in a temporal way you may have prospered, and may be surrounded by comforts and by friends who respect and love you, yet I know that I can call your conscience to witness that in drifting away from God you have drifted away from peace, and that your heart will know no rest until you are conscious again that it is all right between yourself and God.

There is a classic story of a great Eastern king who was once passing through the land, and heard a shepherd playing upon his reeds. The music of the shepherd was so sweet that it gave joy to the soul of the man laden with care, and he took the shepherd to his palace to make of him a minister of joy. He found him so wise and so resourceful that he clothed him with authority, and made him the man who stood next the king. But the envious tongues that surround a monarch whispered that this man was a traitor. It was noted that each day he retired to his room and sat there alone. The king, resolved to find him plotting, burst open the door—and there sat the man clothed in his ancient shepherd's raiment, with his old shepherd's reeds in his hand, trying to charm back the happiness that lay in the dear and unforgotten days of long ago! Comforts had multiplied, slaves had waited on him, wealth had surrounded him with luxury, but happiness was found when these things were not and his life was simple and full of thanksgiving to God. So I say to you that if you could gather all the wealth and power and pleasures of the world, but in doing so should drift away from God, and away from that simple confidence and love which make it possible for you to look up into your Heavenly Father's face and say with childish confidence, "My Father!" you would be wofully defrauded.

Some of you have drifted far away. You have lost your peace, and you are finding the thirst and the hunger and the ashes of disappointment. But over the waves of life comes Jesus Christ, your Savior. He has seen the hunger of your soul, he has heard your smothered cry for help. He who was lonely so many times during his pilgrimage here on earth has sympathized with the homesickness of your heart. And he comes, strong to deliver and mighty to save. Yield yourself to his keeping now!

THE INSPIRATION OF IMMORTALITY.

"The power of an endless life."—*Heb.* vii. 16 (Rev. Ver.).

I THINK few of us who have been reared in Christian lands, and have had the sunlight of immortal hope always illuminating the very atmosphere we breathe, can understand the marvelous power of this hope in gilding all the joys of common life. And yet many live in the midst of this radiance of immortality as tho there were no Christ who had broken the bands of death and let the glorious sunlight into the darkness of the grave.

The power of the hope of immortality is seen most strongly in the fact that those who are inspired by it live lives that ever grow richer and stronger and more splendid as the years go on. A life given up to worldliness, which draws its sources of supply and its satisfaction and joy entirely from this present life, must, in the very nature of things, become more and more impoverished as the years pass away. To the merely worldly soul one avenue after another of human joy and comfort becomes closed up. All the joys and enlivening sensations that come from childhood and youth—and they are very many and very sweet—must rapidly pass into the realm of memory; and so, one after another, every source of mere earthly delight must lose its power to bestow upon us the good for which we long. Even tho, like Solomon, we retain our faculties, and our wisdom remains with us, and we continue to have power and wealth to serve it, yet the keenness and zest of a life which is drawn merely from the senses vanish with use, until, like that ancient king, we are compelled to admit that all is vanity and vexation of spirit.

A strange thing has just come to light in the city of Palermo, Sicily. A widowed princess and her daughter of twenty years, who is blind, five years ago came into the possession of a great fortune, including a splendid palace in Palermo. This palace is composed of a great central building with two wings. The lady occupied half of the lower story in the center, and lodged in the other half her man of affairs, a well-known business man who was married and the father of four children.

One day, over four years ago, her business agent shut the princess and her daughter under lock and key, after having threatened her with death if she cried out, called for aid, showed herself at the window, or gave any signs of life to the outside world. The poor woman submitted, through fear, and lived thus for four years with her blind daughter, terrorized, almost annihilated, and reduced to a condition of the most frightful misery.

There were, however, all this time, servants at the palace—a coachman, a butler, a gardener, and a chambermaid. The villainous trustee dismissed the chambermaid, changed the servants several times, and intimidated them or bribed them so well that no one betrayed him, not even those whom he had dismissed.

Little by little he took away the furniture in the apartments of the princess, leaving her at last nothing but an old bed of straw that had been in one of the servant's rooms. He himself brought food for her and for her daughter, but in such small quantity that the princess was forced to steal to the window when she saw a servant approaching, and beg for the mercy of a piece of bread.

To all persons who called at the palace it was announced that the princess had gone away without leaving her address, and people in Palermo had long questioned what this prolonged absence could mean. The agent had forced her to give him the right of attorney; he was thus enabled to dispose of her fortune in perfect security.

But at length, a short time since, the unfortunate woman succeeded in getting a letter to a distinguished lawyer in Palermo. She told him of her misery, her prison, the sufferings of herself and her daughter, and begged him to inform the authorities. The lawyer knew that he must act secretly and with the utmost haste. He took the letter to the procurator of police, and the latter gave his orders immediately, without announcing the aim in view. About an hour after noon, one day, the palace of the Carini was suddenly surrounded, and the procurator, followed by an examining magistrate and a score of policemen, opened the door and forced his way into the apartments occupied by the princess.

Nothing can surpass the sadness of the spectacle which met their eyes. The princess and her daughter, dressed in the foulest rags, pale, emaciated, shivering with cold, were found there in their strange dignity, almost naked. The two women, nearly mad at the sight of their deliverers, laughed and wept, but could not articulate a word.

Altho the princess and her daughter were free, and at once took possession of the luxurious rooms of their palace, with unlimited means at their command, they were so overcome with fear through their long imprisonment that they begged to have police stationed at the palace.

Sad and tragic as this story is, it seems to me to be a graphic but not exaggerated illustration of the way worldliness, which shuts the inner eyes of the soul to immortal hope, robs and impoverishes men and women. These women had inherited a great fortune, but were deprived of its use. Steadily, day by day, they were starved and abused, losing all the sweetness and comfort of life, tho they were all the time rich, and their very prison was their palace. And is that not true of those who shut their eyes, or are deceived by the enemy of their soul into giving all their attention and service to this present world? No man, however rich or learned or powerful he may be in this life, has because of that any treasures to carry with him into eternity. In the very nature of things life must get poorer to him all the time, for he must soon go away and leave it all. A worldly, material life, that leaves out God and Christ and heaven, is a fruitless life, because it has no permanent results. For a while, as Dr. Maclaren says, permanent results of a sort do follow everything that men do, for all our actions tend to make character, and they all have a share in fixing that which depends upon character, namely, destiny, both here and yonder. And thus the most fleeting of our deeds, which in one aspect are as transitory as the snow upon the valley when the sun rises, leave everlasting traces upon ourselves and upon our condition. But yet acts concerned with transitory things may have permanent fruit, or may be as transient as the things with which they are concerned. And the difference depends on the spirit in which they are done. If the roots are only in the surface skin of soil, when that is pared off the plant goes. A life that is to be eternal must strike its roots down below the surface, down to the very heart of things. When the roots of our affections and our plans twine themselves around God, then the deeds which blossom from them will bloom in unfading beauty forever.

Can you imagine anything sadder than a man who has lived here in this world for forty, or fifty, or sixty, or seventy years, and has given his whole time up to making money, coining his manhood into gold and silver, laying up no treasures beyond the shores of his earthly life, going up at last empty-handed to the judgment-seat of Christ, and saying with a pauper's whine: "O Lord, I made a big fortune down there in the world when I lived there; but sickness and death came along and carried me away, and I left it all behind me." Or another man, who has been studying into the mysteries of the rocks, or the strata of the earth, or the stars, but has had no time to think about the God who made the stars, standing in the blaze of the judgment to say: "I mastered a science, but one gleam of the light of eternity has antiquated it." Or a politician who has given his very soul to win votes and offices, to get power; who has given his Sundays up to secret caucuses, has been too busy to attend revival meetings or listen to the Word of God because he must stand well with the saloons and the ward-heelers—suppose he gains his prizes and is flattered for a while with applause, what a miserable beggar he is as he stands at last before the great white throne to say: "I gained my prizes, won my aims; but when death touched me they all dropped from my palsied fingers, and here I stand having to say in the most tragic sense, 'Nothing in my hands I bring.'"

But here is another man. Possibly he has not been very successful in this world's achievements. People have always said about him: "He is a most lovable man, with such a sweet Christian spirit, but somehow he never knew how to get on well or lay up much for a rainy day." Death draws near to him and undertakes to loosen his fingers on his treasures, but even death stands back awed and reverential before that man's dying hour, for he carries all his treasures with him. Death, the great custom-house officer, finds the richest treasures not on the dutiable list at a Christian's deathbed. His honesty, his sincere character, his loving spirit, his fellowship with Jesus Christ, his peaceful conscience, his happy heart, his immortal hope, his eternal life are not treasures in death's category. Over his coffin the preacher will read: "Blessed are the dead which die in the Lord; they rest from their labors, and their works do follow them"; and standing before the judgment-seat, Jesus Christ, who once was crowned with thorns but now is crowned with glory, will rise up with outstretched arms to say: "Come, ye blessed of my Father, inherit the kingdom prepared for you from the foundation of the world."

Even childhood is brave when inspired by this power of an endless life. A father was once out late in the evening with his little daughter. The night was very dark, and they had passed through thick woods to the brink of a river. Far away on the opposite shore lights twinkled here and there, in a few scattered houses, and farther off still blazed the bright lamps of the great city to which they were going. The little child was weary and sleepy, and the father held her in his arms while he waited for the ferryman, who was on the other side. At length they saw a little light; nearer and nearer came the sound of the oars, and soon they were safe on the boat.

"Father," said the little girl, "it's very dark, and I can't see the shore. Where are we going?"

"The ferryman knows the way, little one; we will soon be over."

Soon in her home, love welcomed her, and all her fears were gone. Some months passed by, and this same child stood on the brink of a river that is darker and more terrible still. It is the river of death! The same loving father is near her, distressed that his child must cross this river and he not be able to go with her. Forty days and nights he and her mother have watched over her, seeking to save the life of the precious one. For hours she has been slumbering; but just before the morning she suddenly awakens, with the eye bright and every faculty alive.

"Father," she says, "I have come again to the river-side, and am waiting for the ferryman to come and take me across."

With voice choked with a grief that it seemed must break his heart, the father tremblingly inquired, "Does it seem as dark and cold as when we crossed the other river, my child?"

"Oh, no! There is no darkness here; the river is covered with floating silver. The boat coming toward me seems made of solid light, and I am not afraid of the ferryman."

"Can you see over the river, my darling?"

"Oh, yes! there is a great and beautiful city there, all filled with light; and I hear music such as angels make."

"Do you see any one on the other side?"

"Why, yes, yes; I see the most beautiful form, and he beckons me now to come. O ferryman, make haste! I know who it is—it is—it is Jesus, my own blessed Jesus!"

And so the child passed over the river of death, changed to a stream of floating silver, glorified by the presence of the Redeemer.

Come to Christ, and let that glorious power of an endless life begin its career in your soul this very hour!

THE LORD'S SAINTS IN THE DEVIL'S PALACE.

"All the saints salute you, especially they that are of Cæsar's household."—*Phil.* iv. 22 (Rev. Ver.).

THERE is something very gracious in this salutation which Paul conveys from the Christians in Rome to those in Philippi. The chief characteristic of the early Christians which attracted the attention of a pagan world that was full of hate and selfishness was their love toward each other. Indeed, that is the chief characteristic of genuine Christianity everywhere. There is no more significant utterance of Jesus than this: "By this shall all men know that ye are my disciples, if ye have love one to another."

In the early days of Christianity, to become a Christian was to become at once the object of opposition and ofttimes of hatred and persecution. But while trouble came from without, the new convert received a marvelous recompense in the love which he received from within the infant church. As soon as a man embraced Christianity he was regarded as a brother and treated as a brother by every Christian he met. And those Christians in Rome felt that their nearest kith and kin in the bonds of tenderest love and fellowship were among the other followers of Christ in Philippi.

We need to emphasize in our day this characteristic of Christianity. It needs to be forever held in remembrance that the Christian church can not exist and do its rightful work in the world without this spirit. When this spirit of loving fellowship has gone out of it, it becomes merely a philosophical or ethical club from which all divine life and power has disappeared. Christ himself is the center of the Christian fellowship. When each member of a church loves Christ supremely, so that Jesus is enthroned in the heart's affections, all will naturally love each other because of their fellowship in him whom they have crowned in their heart Lord over all. There is something very tender in Christ's promise to those who forsake all for his sake: "There is no man that hath left house, or brethren, or sisters, or father, or mother, or children, or lands, for my sake and the gospel's, but he shall receive an hundredfold now in this time, houses and brethren, and sisters, and mothers, and children, and lands."

The love which we have or do not have for those who are serving him is a certain test by which we may know whether we are indeed Christ's disciples.

"We know that we have passed from death unto life," declares one who stood very near to Jesus, "because we love the brethren: he that loveth not his brother abideth in death." It is very evident that that is the true spirit of Christianity, for one of the marked experiences which we all feel in times of revival, when we become more keenly alive to Christian duty and privilege, when the Holy Spirit shines not only on the Word of God but into our hearts, and we rejoice together over sinners turning to Christ, is that our sense of fellowship and Christian love is always greatly increased. We ought to live in this spirit of loving brotherhood all the time; it certainly is not necessary that we should ever become selfishly and coldly critical of each other. If any heart does not respond to this, and you feel that Christians are no nearer to you because they are Christians, then I implore you that you draw near to God at the mercy-seat and plead for forgiveness and for the awakening in your heart that will make your love for Christ a new inspiration and will bring you closer to all those who sincerely love him.

The main thought, however, to which I wish to call your attention is the unexpected place where these Roman saints are found. Paul says: "All the saints salute you; chiefly they that are of Cæsar's household." The Cæsar to whom Paul refers here was the bloodthirsty Nero, a man who was such a monster of vice and cruelty that he has come down through the centuries as a synonym of everything brutal and infamous in human character. Surely, the most unexpected place on earth to find saints of the Christian sort would be in the palace of a tyrant like that. We all know how the character and spirit of a king, or a president, or the head of an administration or of a house, affects the conduct of those who are dependent upon their master's pleasure for their employment—and in those old and bitter times were dependent for their very lives. And yet we know from Paul's writings that there were not only a few Christians in the household of Nero, but a good many of them. It is a marvelous testimony to the fidelity and devotion of Paul that tho he was only a poor prisoner at Nero's court, whose career was to end there by his being beheaded, he was able by his Christian character and faithfulness to win an ever-widening circle around him to love the Christ who had become the supreme master of his own soul.

In the opening of this letter to the Philippians, Paul expresses himself as fearful lest his friends should think that the afflictions which had come upon him had hindered the progress of the gospel. He assures them that just the opposite effect has been realized: "I would ye should understand, brethren, that the things which happened unto me have fallen out rather unto the furtherance of the gospel; so that my bonds in Christ are manifest in all the palace, and in all other places." And again, he says, speaking of the new converts: "And many of the brethren in the Lord, waxing confident by my bonds, are much more bold to speak the word without fear."

The eloquent Melville, meditating on Paul's triumph in Cæsar's palace, says: "I think upon Rome, the metropolis of the world, upon the haughty Cæsars giving laws to well-nigh all the nations of the earth. Oh, that Christianity might make way into the imperial halls! I should feel as tho it were indeed about to triumph over heathenism, were it to penetrate the palace of Nero. And then I hear that St. Paul is approaching toward Rome—St. Paul, who has carried the gospel to the East and West, the North and South, and everywhere made falsehood quail before truth. My expectations are raised. This great champion of Christianity may succeed where there is most to discourage, and gain over Nero's courtiers, if not Nero himself. But then I hear that St. Paul comes as a prisoner. I see him used as a criminal, and debarred from all opportunity of publishing the gospel to the illustrious and powerful. My hopes are destroyed. The great apostle seems to me completely disarmed; and the picture which I had fondly drawn of Christianity growing dominant through God's blessing on his labors, disappears when I behold him detained in captivity. Alas, for human short-sightedness and miscalculation! Never again let me dare reckon God's servant least powerfully when least visibly instrumental in promoting his cause. St. Paul is a prisoner; he can not go boldly to the court and preach to the mighty; but, in less than two years, he is able to declare, 'My bonds are manifest in all the palace,' and to enumerate among the saints who send greetings to the Philippians, 'chiefly them that are of Cæsar's household.'"

Surely there could not be a more important message for us to-day than the one suggested in this Scripture. We are so likely to be discouraged and ready to give up and do nothing because we are hindered from doing the large things in the brilliant way of which we have dreamed. It is not always the most showy and glittering service which most helps on the kingdom of God. The greatest deeds in the world have been wrought by those who did their best for the great cause that urged them on, and to which they gave their devotion in the midst of severe poverty and discouragement. As Dr. Watkinson so graphically and earnestly says, it takes the world a long time to learn that it is not the size of a man's purse, nor the size of his body, nor the size of his earthly power of any kind, but it is the size of a man's soul, the depth of his devotion and love, that counts most. The little goes a long way when managed by a great-souled and heroic nature. "Out of my poverty have I done this," said Turner, when he had painted his great masterpiece out of broken tea-cups. Christopher Columbus did not discover America in one of the great steam ferries that cross the Atlantic in a week, but he pushed his way by his enthusiasm and his devotion in a boat in which you would not be willing to risk yourself out of sight of land on Lake Erie. Through blindness John Milton gave us "Paradise Lost." Within prison walls John Bunyan gave us "Pilgrim's Progress," that has led thousands out of the City of Destruction, up from the Slough of Despond, and onward to the Palace Beautiful and the streets of gold.

I would to God we might all understand that in this present campaign which we are making in this church to win multitudes of souls to Christ, it is first and last and all the time personal consecration to the Lord and his work which we need. It is not a question of strength or eloquence or position. It is a question of love, faith, hope, devotion, and of a soul on fire to kindle abroad love for Christ. It is only with these weapons that we can do great and marvelous works in seeking after the lost and winning them to our Lord.

I return again to put emphasis on the fact that it is not the most brilliant gift that may be the most serviceable. I noticed the other day that the United States Government had decided not to wait for reindeer as means of transportation from the seaboard to the Klondike in carrying food to the miners. It seems it has been impossible for the government agents to get these animals from Lapland in time to be of service this winter. It is the present purpose of the War Department to push through with mule pack-trains as far as possible, leaving the reindeer to follow up the trail if they come along at all. A mule is not by any means as aristocratic an animal as the reindeer, but when there is some hard work to be done, requiring fidelity and endurance, he is a remarkably serviceable beast. I often think, when present at great conventions and dress parades of the Christian church, that modern Christianity has all the reindeer it needs, but there is always room for those who are glad to be even the Lord's mules, and in fellowship with Jesus Christ carry burdens and pull loads if perchance through his grace they may help to bring the Bread of Life within the reach of those who are starving in the cold, dark mountains of sin.

The secret of Paul's joy and gladness even when his hands were chained to his guard in prison was in the fact that he knew he was a serviceable Christian and was doing the work of Christ. Paul loved Christ so much that it was his greatest mission in life to spread abroad the good news of the Lord. Prisons, chains, stripes were all the same as palaces to Paul if all the time he was preaching Christ and winning those who were brought into contact with him to know the same heavenly joy that had come to his own heart. This secret of Paul's joyous experience in the midst of hardship is an open secret, and you and I may act upon it and enjoy the same glorious results in our own lives. If any of you have been excusing yourselves from earnest effort for the salvation of souls because you are getting old, or you are poor, or your hands are tied by business engagements, I beg you to contrast yourself with Paul. Here was such an one who was "Paul the aged." And tho we have reason to believe that he was once wealthy, he was now so poor that he had to send word to a friend to bring an old cloak that had been left on his travels, because he shivered with cold in his dungeon. One hand was chained to the hand of the soldier who guarded him. But under such circumstances Paul made no excuses; he so gave his heart and life up to prayer to God and to conversations about Jesus, and lived the gospel so enthusiastically and sweetly before those who saw him, that a Roman soldier could not be chained to him without finding Paul's religion contagious, and becoming himself converted to Christ.

I want by God's grace to speak a word in season to any that have once known the Lord, but have grown weary and fallen out by the way. Some who hear me have, it may be, in other towns or cities, been open and earnest disciples of Christ, but coming into new surroundings you have failed to identify yourself with the kingdom of God here, and tho you still keep up, possibly, a form of religion, the vital fire which once flamed on the altar of your heart has died down to ashes.

It has recently been decided to have an auction of schoolhouses in Western Kansas. The state officials have ordered that schoolhouses in depopulated districts, which are not in use, may be sold to the highest bidder. There are more than one hundred of these buildings scattered over the prairies, abandoned except as an abode for bats and owls. They are decaying and crumbling. Are there here those whose hearts were once the abode of Jesus Christ, where many a feast of divine fellowship was held, where often the heart burned within as the great Teacher sat and opened unto you the Scriptures; but your coldness and your neglect have driven him away from your heart, and now the owls and bats of indifference and worldliness have taken possession, and all your soul fabric is crumbling and decaying because of your thoughtless and sinful life? If such is your sad case to-day, I pray that you will in penitence and faith implore again the coming of the Redeemer. Tho you have slighted him, and treated him as you would no other friend, yet his love is so great that he will come back even now and bring to you again the joy of his forgiving love.

And some of you who have never known the Lord should take courage from this brave and noble spirit and volunteer this day to be a soldier of Jesus Christ. Gen. O. O. Howard, a most devout and beloved Christian man as well as a brave officer, has recently told an interesting story of his conversion. He one day sat in uniform on a back seat in a small church. A little colored boy who sat beside him fell asleep, and rested his head on the General's breast. He was proud and sensitive and did not like the situation, but he always had a tender heart for children. It was in a time of revival, and the preacher came down the aisle speaking to one and another, asking them to go to the altar and seek Christ. Finally he came up to the young officer with a personal appeal. "Which side would you rather be on, the Lord's side, or the side of those who reject Christ?" the preacher said. Promptly and resolutely the General's heart answered: "The Lord's side"; and he arose, buttoned up his military coat, and marched down the aisle to the altar, where he humbly knelt and committed himself to Christ. He did not at first find the light, but when he went back to his quarters he picked up "The Life of Hedley Vicars." He read it with deep interest. He could not understand what was meant by the saying, so oft repeated: "The blood of Jesus Christ, his Son, cleanseth us from all sin." He knelt down and asked God to show him what it meant, and God did show him. His soul was filled with unspeakable joy. Soon after this General Howard went to the war, and he says that on the eve of his first battle he became pale and weak at the sound of cannon and musketry and the roar of conflict. But he cried out to God to give him strength to do his duty, and quick as a flash his courage and strength came and he never faltered again in the face of any peril. One day his dear friend, Captain Griffith, was shot down on the field of Gettysburg, and the General helped to bear him a little way back from the battle to die. He read at his friend's side the sweet words of Jesus: "Let not your heart be troubled: . . . in my Father's house are many mansions: if it were not so, I would have told you. I go to prepare a place for you. And if I go and prepare a place for you, I will come again, and receive you unto myself; that where I am, there ye may be also." At these words the dying captain lifted his eyes to those of his friend and said: "General Howard, I am not afraid to die. I am ready to go!" Ah, that is the way Christian soldiers can live and die.

In the name of my Lord, this day, I call upon you to volunteer as the soldier of Jesus Christ!

THE STORY OF A SHIPWRECK.

"This charge I commit unto thee, my child Timothy, according to the prophecies which went before on thee, that by them thou mayest war the good warfare; holding faith and a good conscience; which some having thrust from them made shipwreck concerning the faith: of whom is Hymenæus and Alexander."—1 *Tim.* i. 18-20 (Rev. Ver.).

THERE is something very beautiful in Paul's letter to this young man, Timothy, in the reference which he makes to his living up to the prophecies which have been made concerning him. Paul is not referring here to any Scripture prophecies made in the Old Testament, but he no doubt alludes to the hopes which his mother and his relatives and friends had for him, and the dreams which they entertained of the strong and noble man he was some day to be. It is a great thing to be born in a Christian home and grow up surrounded by loving prophecies that plan for us a life pure and noble. To have good people believing in him is a great bulwark to a young man, and a youth must be very hard-hearted indeed who can falsify all the prophecies of a good mother or a noble father, and cause all their dreams to come to naught, without deepest sorrow and anguish

Yet many that have gone down to the depths of sorrow and despair have had loving prophecies made about them in their youth, as splendid as any concerning those who have climbed the heights of noblest triumph. Hartley Coleridge, the son of the greater Samuel Taylor Coleridge, inherited from his father the moral blight of a weakened and vicious will, and instead of fighting it in the strength of God he gave himself over to the bondage of the destroying appetite for strong drink. His life was a failure, and in later years he wrote these sad and pathetic lines on the fly-leaf of a Bible given to him when he was but a youth:

"When I received this volume small,
  My years were barely seventeen,
When it was hoped I should be all
  Which once, alas! I might have been.

"And now my years are thirty-five;
  And every mother hopes her lamb,
And every happy child alive,
  May never be what now I am."

If there are those who hear me who have been untrue to the prophecies and hopes and dreams of those who loved you most tenderly in your childhood and youth, I pray God you may come back to the Christ who is able to save you even now!

It is interesting to notice what Paul regarded as

the equipment necessary for warring a good warfare, and the making a safe journey of the voyage of life. "Holding faith and a good conscience." Conscience is the compass to direct the ship's course, and faith the sails that are to drive her on her way. No ship is ready to go to sea that lacks either compass or sails. What a fool a captain would be who would allow anybody to interfere with the perfect condition of his compass! but he would be less foolish than the man who is untrue to his conscience. A man who stands faithful to his conscience has always God's voice in his heart to tell him which way to steer. Better lose your position, better lose any temporary success, than to warp or destroy in any way your conscience.

There was an Irish boy whose master wished to lengthen a web that was short measure. He gave the boy one end, and took hold of the other himself. He then said, "Pull, Adam, pull!" but the boy stood still. "Pull, Adam!" he shouted again. But the boy said, "I can't, sir."

"Why not?" the master asked.

"My conscience will not allow me."

"You will never do for a linen manufacturer," the master replied.

That boy became the famous Dr. Adam Clarke, and persuaded tens of thousands of men to hold faith and a good conscience. Though he is dead, like Abel he yet speaks all the world round for righteousness.

Faith and a good conscience steady the soul in the time of peril. A few weeks ago the rain which fell upon the tracks and the car decks of the Mountain division of the Pennsylvania railroad was turned into ice almost instantly. This rendered both tracks and cars unusually dangerous, and the descent of the steep grade between Gallitzin and Altoona was attended by imminent peril. A big mogul engine, hauling forty-three heavily laden cars, passed through the tunnel at Gallitzin and began to descend the mountain. Soon after leaving the tunnel, the engineer saw that the train was beginning to move very rapidly. He applied the air-brakes, but as that did not perceptibly reduce the speed, he whistled "down brakes." Still the terrible speed increased, and the long train swept around the "Horseshoe curve" at the rate of sixty miles an hour. The men expected to be hurled into the abyss, but the train rounded the sharp curves and rushed on with ever-increasing speed till it crashed into another freight train in Altoona. The engineer and his fireman went down in the wreck, and the *débris* of the cars and their contents were piled thirty feet above them. Strangely enough, neither was much hurt, and both men were able to crawl from beneath the towering ruins.

The first thing these two men, who had been facing death all the way down the mountain, did after they emerged from the wreck was to drop on their knees on the track and thank God for their preservation. Men ordinarily careless and indifferent stood awed and deeply impressed before their reverent worship. The engineer has been for years an earnest Christian man. It was his faith in God and his good conscience that enabled him to sit with his hand upon the throttle, calmly awaiting what seemed to him the inevitable end. When the newspaper men interviewed him in his home, he was remarkably tranquil, and said with modest humility: "The religion of the Lord Jesus Christ is a splendid possession in the moment of dire peril."

There is no danger of shipwreck so long as we hold fast to faith in God and a conscience void of offense toward God and man. All heaven guards the soul that is thus equipped. I have been reading recently, in a story by Mark Guy Pearse, an incident which I have often experienced myself at sea, when lying in my berth in the stillness of the night, hundreds or possibly thousands of miles from the nearest land. When the waves were tossing against the side of the ship, just outside, like living things impatient of their prey, I would hear the bells ring out the hour, and the strokes repeated by the lookout man on the bow, followed by a cheerful cry, "All's well; lights burning bright." And then down amidships another man would repeat the strokes, and back again would come the cry "All's well." There is no sweeter note at sea than that. The passenger that hears it turns over in his berth to go to sleep again in confidence. "All's well; lights burning bright"—so long as we keep our faith in God and our conscience true, those are the cheery words that come to us amid all the storms of life.

How is it with you to-night? Have you the witness in your own heart that all is well? If you can not say promptly that this is so, then you must know that it is not all well, and you need to come closer to Christ. Suppose you were at sea on an ocean unknown to you, and some night you should meet one of the officers and inquire "Is all well?" and he should reply, "Well, I hope so." You would be alarmed in a moment. You would never be satisfied with an answer like that. You would at once understand that he really meant "I am afraid not." And so sometimes at the door of this church, as I shake hands with the people coming in, I inquire of a man or a woman, "Are you a Christian?" And they hesitate, and say, "I don't know." I am alarmed at once, for I know that down in their hearts they feel that they are not. They are on an unknown ocean, far from the port, and have lost hold of faith and a good conscience. Do not go on in such a condition as that, for God is able and willing to come into your life and take full possession of your heart, and give you to know the gladness of your salvation.

You may be very sure that if you are in doubt about your relation to God, it is not well with you, and you have every reason to be alarmed. A traveler, telling the story of a voyage, said that once the officers of the ship could not take the reckonings in the storm, and supposed that they were off a notoriously rough headland. It was blowing a hurricane right ashore, and the traveler asked one of the officers where they were. He said he did not know exactly, but that they had turned the ship right out to sea. All night the captain was on the deck; and all night the lead was being flung out and the depth taken. They knew well enough within a few miles where they were; but that would not do. With the shore not far away, a little distance might make all the difference between safety and shipwreck. So if you do not know where you are, I beg you lift up your hearts to the great Pilot that he may come aboard and take possession of your storm-tossed ship. Christ, our guide and captain, who knows the way, is ready to come and bring us safely to the haven of rest. If you will confess him, and rest in him, you may go to sleep with the glad cry ringing in your ears, "All's well; lights burning bright!"

We do not know just what it was that led these two men, Hymenæus and Alexander, to lose hold of their good conscience and faith and make the awful shipwreck about which Paul writes. Perhaps they formed bad associations, where their religion was sneered at, and they held back from fellowship with the people of God until after a while they became ashamed themselves of their friendship for Christ. I have known people to allow their religion to be undermined in that way. Sometimes young people, who have never thought about being ashamed of Christ in their old home, come up to the big city, and in the boarding-house or in the store or the office they run across an atmosphere that is full of sneers at Christianity and Christian people. If they would speak right out bravely and stand up for Christ with loyalty, they would win the admiration and respect of these very people, and would possibly win them to accept Jesus; but by keeping still and failing to show their colors they soon make shipwreck of what faith they have.

Perhaps these men had only a theoretical faith

in Christ. They had heard about him and had watched the remarkable transformation that had come over some of their friends who had become Christians, and when anybody asked them if they believed in Christ they said, "Oh: certainly, I believe in Christ. I know he is able to save." But when they were pressed to put their faith into their life and really come to Christ, and take him as their Savior, they hesitated and delayed about it, until after a while they grieved away the Holy Spirit and were lost in shipwreck.

It is not enough to have a theoretical faith in Jesus. One must have an acting faith that really comes to Christ. There must be a distinct coming to Christ, a renouncing of sin, and obedience to God. It is not the people who admire Christ, or who have a theoretical faith in him, and, it may be, say many pleasant things about him, whom Christ promises to save; it is those who actually come to him. This is his promise: "Him that cometh to me I will in no wise cast out." Thomas Spurgeon says that that promise is the sheet-anchor of the sinner's hope of salvation. Suppose there is out here in the lake a storm-tossed ship. The captain has lost control of her, and she seems certain to drift ashore. One anchor after another is thrown over without success. She still drifts. The anchors will not hold. Finally, they throw out the sheet-anchor, and you watch anxiously. Presently the motion of the ship seems stayed a little, and after a while she brings up suddenly and is held fast, and the people who are about you cry out: "It holds! It holds!" Ah, often I have seen this in spiritual matters. I have seen many a man who was convicted of his sin, and who felt that he had lost the control over his life, and that he was steadily drifting toward the rocks and certain disaster. I have seen such a man throw out one anchor after another. I have seen him sign the pledge, or change his employment, or go to a new town that he might be under different surroundings; but the anchors would not hold. I talked with a man the other day who sobbed and cried as tho his heart would break as he told me that his sins had caused him to leave his home in old England and come over here, hoping he might get away from the old associations and have sailing room for a new chance, but he said, as he sobbed in despair: "I've fallen into the old sin here! what shall I do? what shall I do? My father and mother are broken-hearted, and I hate my sin, and yet I drift right back into it again! what shall I do?" I have seen men like that, when every anchor had dragged, finally persuaded to cast out "The Sinner's Sheet-Anchor," and come to Jesus Christ, and give him their whole hearts. And I have seen the joy in the faces of their friends as well as in their own as they have shouted "It holds! It holds!" I offer you "The Sinner's Sheet-Anchor" to-night. It is not my word. It is the word of him who spake as never man spake. It is the word of him who has all power to keep his promise unto your salvation. Hear him, and act upon it, here and now. "Him that cometh to me I will in no wise cast out."

CHRIST'S CONQUERING HEROES.

"In all these things we are more than conquerors through him that loved us."—*Rom.* viii. 37 (Rev. Ver.).

THREE very striking and significant phrases are contained in this text. The first is in the words, "these things." The things specified are in the verses immediately preceding and immediately following this one. To appreciate them, the paragraph must be taken entire: "Who shall separate us from the love of Christ? shall tribulation, or anguish, or persecution, or famine, or nakedness, or peril, or sword? . . . Nay, in all these things we are more than conquerors through him that loved us. For I am persuaded, that neither death, nor life, nor angels, nor principalities, nor things present, nor things to come, nor powers, nor height, nor depth, nor any other creature, shall be able to separate us from the love of God, which is in Christ Jesus our Lord."

Now these are things we know about. They are things with which every one of us has to deal; for, however far away some of them may seem now, it is impossible to go through this world without having to do with tribulation and anguish, and ofttimes with poverty and with many and unforeseen perils. Some of you have to meet these things this very moment. The troubles of life are universal. Their seeds are in the very air we breathe, and we have to struggle with them as best we may. Paul says that in Jesus Christ is found divine help that can give us the power to overcome them and come off victorious. In another place Paul declares that Jesus Christ is able to help us, and comfort us, and intercede for us before the throne of God, because he knows our troubles and sorrows, having gone through them himself. In order that he might become the Captain of our salvation, he was perfected through suffering. For thirty-three years he lived in the midst of this human life, experienced its poverty, was the object of suspicion and envy and jealousy and hatred, was insulted and abused, went hungry and thirsty, was lonesome and homesick, was beaten with stripes, was deserted by his friends, was plotted against by wicked enemies, was betrayed to death by a bosom companion, and was tempted in all points like as we are. Surely we can all see that this fits Jesus Christ to be our best friend and helper in the hard places of life. There is nothing better than a like experience to make us able to help another who is in trouble.

A traveler in Switzerland, in writing of his experiences in that country, gives a very beautiful incident. The window of a little shop in an old arcade in Berne was filled one day with crosses and hearts intended for the decoration of graves, and among them were several slabs of marble, with the inscription, "In memory of my sister," and other similar sentiments. A number of tourists had halted to laugh at what they called the uncultivated taste shown in these cheap votive offerings. Apart, and quite unconscious of them, stood a poor Swiss maid-servant. Her eyes were full of eager longing and the tears slowly ran down her cheeks. The slab which she coveted was the cheapest and poorest of the lot, a black slab, white-lettered; but the inscription was, "To my dear mother."

"She stops every morning to look at that," whispered the shopkeeper. "But she won't have enough money to buy it in years."

"Tell her she can have it," said one of the tourists, a well-dressed man, in a loud voice. "I'll pay for it."

"Monsieur is very generous," answered the shopkeeper. "But I doubt—she is no beggar."

While they were speaking, a young American girl, who, with sympathy expressed in her face, had been watching the woman, drew her aside.

"I am a stranger." she said. "I have been very

happy in Berne. I am going away to-morrow, never to come back again. I should like to think somebody here would remember me kindly. Will you not let me give you that little slab to lay on your mother's grave?"

The woman's face was filled with amazement, and then with delight. The tears rained down her cheeks. She grasped the girl's hand in both of her own.

"You, too, have lost your mother? Yes? Then you can understand! I thank you, gracious lady."

Ah, it was the experience back of the sympathy and the kind deed that made it possible for the young woman for the moment to personate Jesus Christ, her Lord, as the comforter of the sad-hearted stranger. What we can do imperfectly at best, Jesus can do perfectly; for while he came out from them without sin, without spot on his garments, he yet knows the terrible temptations through which we have to go.

The second impressive phrase is, "More than conquerors." I think that seems a little exaggerated at first. We say to ourselves, How can one be more than a conqueror? But that all clears away with a little reflection. One may be a conqueror, and yet at a fearful cost. There have been many times when a general has won a victory and held the battle-field, while his enemy was compelled to retreat, and yet felt that his victory was almost worse than defeat—it had cost so heavily. But when we win a victory without any loss at all —that is, losing nothing that is of any value to us —then surely we are more than conquerors. Here is the gold that is brought out of the mine in dirt and rock, where its beauty, usefulness, and glory have been hidden away for thousands of years; and it goes through the crusher, and the shaking-table, and the furnace, and under the die, and comes out a shining gold coin with the face of a queen, or with the American eagle and the symbol of liberty upon it. It might as well talk of what it has lost, as for a sinner to talk about what he has to give up, or lose, to become a Christian. From the time the miner's pick or blast dug the gold out in broken rock until it lies on the bank-counter a shining coin, it has never lost anything except its dirt and its dross. And so from the time the sinner is convicted of his sin, and his hard heart is hammered to pieces by the Word of God, and he is drawn toward the mercy-seat by the loving invitations of Jesus, until he stands with joyous face and glad heart confessing Christ as his Savior and Lord, the only thing he has to lose is his dross and the dirt of his sin. Surely he is more than conqueror.

Perhaps there is another way in which this phrase ought to be emphasized for the comfort and encouragement of those who long to be Christians, and yet are afraid to start because they fear they will not be able to hold true to their profession of Christ. Surely in Paul's promise that comes in, and Paul ought to be a good witness. Not one of you will have to fight such battles as Paul had to encounter. Suppose your becoming a Christian meant that you must start out to face mobs, and be beaten and stoned until you were unconscious, and picked up for dead in the streets; and, in the next town, be taken up and whipped at the public whipping-post because of your Christian faith; and in the next place, after having been beaten by the mob until you were torn and bleeding, be thrust, supperless, into the inner prison, with your feet in the stocks, to lie there on the stone floor. Suppose that, in the first large city you reach, they would take you and put you in a stall, like a wild beast, and make you fight with a lion, life for life, in the dust and blood of the arena, for the idle amusement of a brutal crowd. Paul went through that, and that is the sort of man who writes this promise. He knew what he was talking about. How insignificant, after all, seem all the foes you have to face compared to what this man had been through and experienced when he says, "In all these things we are more than conquerors."

I am not asking you, however, to undertake the

Christian life in your own strength, and that brings me to call your particular attention to the third emphatic phrase of the text. Paul's basis of glorious conquest is that we shall be more than conquerors "through him that loved us." A man can do all things when once he gets it down into his heart that the divine Christ loves him and will stand by him to the end! I have read you that old, old, yet ever new, story of the prodigal as our Scripture lesson. Did you notice that it was when the prodigal began to think of his father, and remembered—what he had forgotten for a long time —how his father loved him, that he "came to himself"? Mark Guy Pearse says that he found the father's love, and then he found himself. Before it was, "I am lost"; now it is, "I am loved." While he was feeding the swine and eating the husks and thinking sadly of the mean way in which the people who had eaten his suppers and drank his wine had treated him when he lost his money, he was saying about himself, "I am nothing to anybody"; but now when he stops to think about his father, he says, "I am something to him —to him I am much, I am everything. He would rather see me come than the richest man in the country. Mean as I've been to him, he loves me." And he arose and went to his father. So long as you hang back and think about your sins, and remember what miserable work you have made of trying to do right in your own strength, and reflect only on the meanness of sinful humanity, it is no wonder you are discouraged, and say, "There's no use of my starting! I wouldn't stick. I couldn't carry on a Christian life among the people where I work," and all that sort of despairing talk. But if you'll turn about face and stop looking at yourself, and look to Jesus and remember that he loves you, you will be uplifted and will be ready to say with Paul in his letter to the Philippians: "I can do all things through Christ which strengtheneth me." You see what a tremendous ally you have. The moment you give yourself to Christ, no matter how poor and helpless you feel, you have his fresh and glorious strength added to yours. Ah, that's the blessed privilege of our humanity—that we may take hold upon him as our strength.

Do not reject this divine help which he offers you. Do not grieve the loving heart of him who comes with outstretched hand to lead you out of your weakness and your sin to glorious victory.

THE GREAT WRESTLING MATCH.

"Abhor that which is evil; cleave to that which is good."
—*Rom.* xii. 9 (Rev. Ver.).

"Be not overcome of evil, but overcome evil with good."
—*Rom.* xii. 21 (Rev. Ver.).

THESE two texts properly belong together, and they reveal to us how clear to Paul's mind was the antipathy between good and evil. No possible compromise can be made between them. A man can not hold on to both sides. Christ says we can not serve God and Mammon, speaking of only one phase of evil. It is just as true to say that we can not serve good and evil, putting it in the broadest sense. No man can serve two masters, says Christ. Anybody that undertakes it will soon find that one of them comes into supremacy. He will hate the one and love the other, or cleave to the one and despise the other.

Tremendously strong words are these which Paul uses to show the intensity of the warfare which is constantly going on between the good and evil. It is not enough for us simply to be neutral;

we should be just as positive in our cleaving to the good as we are in abhorring the evil. There is something intense and cutting, like a sword, in the separation indicated between these two words. We are to abhor that which is evil. That is the beginning of a Christian life. A man abhors his sins before he loves righteousness. The word "abhor" is no feeble word. Put disgust and hate and indignation and contempt all together and shake them up, and you can get that word abhor; and yet a great many men abhor their sins and are not saved. I have seen a man who so loathed his sin that its horrible character was ever before him, and he could not think of it or hear it spoken of without hanging his head in shame, and yet he went on committing it. Thousands of men go down to eternal darkness abhorring and loathing the sins that have robbed them of their peace and led them, miserable slaves, to destruction. One must not only abhor his sins, but turn from them, and cease to do them by filling the mind and heart with something to take their place; which brings in the other side of the picture, "Cleave to that which is good." That word "cleave" means not simply shaking hands. It is the grasp with which a drowning man seizes and holds the life-line that is thrown him from the shore or the ship. It is the grasp with which a mother holds her child when in the midst of some sudden peril. "Cleave to that which is good."

Between these two qualities, good and evil, there is a wrestling match in every human life. We can not be neutral. We are called upon by the Word of God not simply to stand on the defensive, but to take the aggressive and overcome the evil with the good. That is possible in every human soul. There never yet was a man so placed, or so constituted, that the aggressive good which he is able to draw to his aid in Jesus Christ, his Savior, was not, and is not, strong enough to attack and overcome all the evil of his nature and all the evil forces that can be brought against him.

Some of you stand at a very critical time in the story of your life. You are drawn both ways. There are many things that are influencing you toward evil, while on the other hand Christ is knocking at the door of your heart and the Holy Spirit is drawing you toward the good. You have been rather indifferent, and have tried to escape an earnest life-and-death grapple between the good and the evil. But you can not escape from such a struggle. If you just let it alone and let matters take their course, the evil is absolutely certain to overcome the good, and you will be given over to everlasting defeat. All that can save you from disaster is that you shall arouse yourself from this lethargy, and by accepting Christ as your Savior positively and aggressively "cleave to that which is good."

I have been very much interested recently in an account given by Rev. Dr. George F. Pentecost of the conversion of his son. The young man had been studying in Germany, and had become very skeptical in regard to the Christian truth which was so dear to his father and mother, and which in his childhood he had never doubted. His father was a pastor in London, and the young man, tho in business, lived at home. He finally stayed away from the church services, and for many months had not listened to a sermon. There came a time when his father saw that he was very restless and unhappy, and felt that a momentous struggle was going on in the boy's heart, which would probably decide whether he would ever become a Christian or not. During these days the father and mother gave themselves up largely to secret prayer on his behalf.

One evening, in the week before Communion Sunday, Dr. Pentecost was reading and his son was sitting on the other side of the open grate fire with his face buried in his hands—a favorite position of his when in thought. Presently the doctor was aroused by his son's saying:

"Father, what are the conditions necessary

to qualify one for coming to the Lord's Supper?"

He was somewhat surprised at this question from his son; but regarding it for a moment as but a passing thought, he replied without looking in his direction:

"Why, the conditions necessary to partake of the Lord's Supper are just those that are necessary to partake of life in him. Whatever puts one into union with Christ qualifies him to show forth that union in the celebration of the Supper. In other words: 'If you believe on the Lord Jesus Christ and heartily accept him as your Savior and Lord, you are qualified to eat of the Supper.'"

While he was making this answer, Dr. Pentecost began to wonder why his son had asked such a question, and especially after a half-hour of silence. The question must have arisen out of his present thoughts, and they must have been in the direction of his question. So he turned and faced the boy, who was still sitting with elbows on his knees, and face buried in his hands.

"Why, my boy, do you ask this question—generally, in respect of other people, or are you speaking for yourself?"

At this the young man lifted up his face from his hands and looked at his father. The tears were coursing down his cheeks, and he said, with a broken voice: "Well, father, I can not live as I have been living. It is not good enough, and I am tired of it. I must either give myself to God, or I must go straight to the devil. The ground I am living on now is not tenable, and I can not stay long where I am. So I say, I must either give myself to God or go straight to the devil."

"Tell me, my dear boy, just what you mean by that," the father replied, with his heart in his throat.

"Well, you know about what kind of a life I have been living for the past year or two. I have not gone far toward the bad, but have just been living for the passing hour and such pleasures as I could get out of a respectable life, on the edges of a world of sin and wickedness into which I have not yet gone. As I have said, the life I am now living is not good enough. It bores me terribly. To go over wholly to the world I can see plainly means ruin. There is no other place to go unless one goes over to God. Therefore I say I must either give myself to God or go to the devil. I am frank to confess that there is much in the life of the world which I have not seen or tasted which attracts and fascinates me; but I know that such a life would mean death and ruin. On the other hand, I must confess that the Christian life does not much appeal to me, it does not attract me, except that I know it is the right life."

"Well, my boy," the father answered, "go on and talk out all your heart to me. You know how gladly I will help you if I can. You can not doubt that my whole heart is in deepest sympathy with you in this struggle."

"Well, father, you know that I have been somewhat skeptical about many things connected with the Bible and Christianity. I have never doubted the existence of God, and I do not think I have really doubted, at least I have certainly never so disbelieved the general facts of Christianity as to call myself an infidel. The whole matter of Christ's coming, his death and resurrection, and salvation in him, is not clear to me. I do not know whether I believe or not. But, father, I believe in you and mother; and you believe in God and in Christ, and are Christians; and if you think God will take me just as I am, I am ready to give myself to him. I am very sinful and very weak and very ignorant; and I am not at all sure that I can live a consistent Christian life. I can not go on as I am; I do not want to go to the bad; I am persuaded that I ought to follow Christ; and after all I have told you, if you think he will take me, I am ready to surrender now."

No words can ever describe the joy of that

father's heart as he assured his son that the blessed Lord was glad to have him just as he was; that he can take us in no other way; that it is our sin and our ignorance and our weakness which appeal to him, and that he only waits for a willing heart and mind in men; that "he is able to save unto the uttermost" and "keep from falling" all those who come to him.

The father proposed that they should kneel down and talk it all out to God. They did so, and he prayed, thanking God for his goodness in bringing his dear son to himself; for all the way he had led him; for all the patient, loving kindness of his grace, and for that happy hour; and asking that he would keep him in the hollow of his hand and guide him into that way of life he would have him go.

Then the boy prayed for himself. With broken voice he poured out his heart to God in confession, and besought Jesus to forgive all his sins, and to help him to live for his glory, to do some work for him, and be a help to "my father."

When they arose from their knees and looked each other in the face, the relationship of father and son was for a moment lost in a new kinship—they were brothers in Christ.

After the boy had gone to bed, Dr. Pentecost hastened to the mother's room, and, tho he found her asleep, he wakened her and told her the good news. Far into the night he heard the soft crying of that mother over her son's return. They were tears of gladness and joy, and he did not disturb their flow.

The following Sunday the young man came with his mother and sister to the communion. He at once told his nearest companions of the step he had taken. Two or three of them followed him into the church at the succeeding communion.

And now here is a matter which I wish specially to emphasize for the benefit of any young man whom the devil may have led to believe that a genuine outspoken Christianity and an enthusiasm for the work of the Lord would harm him in his business life. A few months after his son's conversion, Dr. Pentecost happened to meet the man under whom the son was getting his training for his technical profession. The gentleman remarked to the doctor: "Do you know that during the last few months the most wonderful change has come over your son? I was really fearing that he would not do. Not that he neglected his work, but that it seemed to bore him. He took no interest in it apparently, and was only anxious to get his daily task done. He would always do faithfully, and fairly well, what he was bidden to do, but that was all. His manners, never impolite, were taciturn, and when he came to the office it was barely a 'good morning.' But now he seems to have suddenly waked up, and is throwing himself into his work with an enthusiasm that is delightful to see; and he is so very pleasant. It is really a pleasure to have him come in, and his 'good morning' is a real refreshment. I never saw such a change in a boy. I can't make out what has come over him."

"Well, Mr. M., I can tell you all about it. My boy has recently been converted—born again; and what you have noticed is the fruit of the Spirit working out in his life."

The worldly minded man of business, who was not a Christian, looked puzzled for a moment, and then said: "I don't know anything about what you call the new birth and being converted, but I know that your boy is wonderfully changed in the last few months, and is a great delight to us all in the office."

May this story be blessed by the Holy Spirit unto the salvation of some of you who stand in the same place where this boy stood! Your life needs the divine tonic of a hope from heaven that shall awaken you to do the best which, by the help of the grace of God, it is possible for you to do. Yield your heart to that divine inspiration now!

THE CREDENTIALS OF LOVE.

"For while we were yet weak, in due season Christ died for the ungodly. For scarcely for a righteous man will one die: for peradventure for a good man some would even dare to die. But God commendeth his own love toward us, in that, while we were yet sinners, Christ died for us."
—*Rom.* v. 6-8 (Rev. Ver.).

CREDENTIALS stand for a great deal in our modern life. An ambassador goes from the court of his native land to the seat of government in some distant empire, and is received with all honor because of the credentials he bears. A man comes into a business house, and on the faith which is put in the credentials he carries, business transactions of great moment are discussed and determined with him. The Scriptures set forth the credentials of the love of God in Jesus Christ. There certainly can be no more interesting subject, for our destiny must forever hang on the disposition of God's heart toward us. John, who was so near to Christ and whose heart was so susceptible to divine teaching, declares that "God is love" in the very essence of his being. And Paul assures us that love is one of the three graces of the soul that is to abide when all else passes away. The poet has Scriptural authority to sing:

> "They sin who tell us love can die;
> With life all other passions fly,—
>   All others are but vanity.
> In heaven ambition can not dwell,
> Nor avarice in the vaults of hell;
> Earthly, these passions of the earth,
> They perish where they had their birth,
>   But love is indestructible.
> Its holy flame forever burneth:
> From heaven it came, to heaven returneth.
> Too oft on earth a troubled guest,
> At times deceived, at times oppressed,
>   It here is tried and purified,
> Then hath in heaven its perfect rest.
> It serveth here with toil and care
> But the harvest-time of love is there."

Our text declares that God's love has gone forth in sacrifice and service with all the divine graciousness of the heaven from whence it came.

It is hard to find illustrations that will faintly suggest the depth and strength of the love of Christ, even in a world where love is so great a factor. A touching incident occurred recently in Poland. A peasant and his wife, residing in a village near Warsaw, had gone to attend a wedding at a neighboring village. It became very cold during the night, and they were unable to get back until morning. They had left their dwelling in the care of two little boys, one about six years of age, and his brother, two years younger. It appears that near nightfall these two boys had gone out to amuse themselves in the falling snow. During the time they were playing, the front door had become so frozen in its place that on their return they were unable to open it and gain access to their home. They could not endure the severe cold, and were frozen to death. When the bodies of the little victims to their parents' carelessness and the bitter night were found, it was noticed that the elder had made, in tender solicitude, every effort to save the younger. He had taken off his shoes and put them over the felt shoes of his little brother, leaving himself barefooted, and had clasped him to his bosom in a rigid embrace. All had been in vain. They both lay in the stronger embrace of death, their cheeks covered with frozen tears.

Of course no one could contemplate such self-sacrifice as that practised by the heroic elder brother without the most heartfelt admiration; and yet it was his brother for whom he was doing it, who all his little life, no doubt, had been full of comfort and sunshine to him. It was, after all, only love responding back to love again. "But God commendeth his own love toward us, in that, while we were yet sinners, Christ died for us." Was there ever love like that?

Henry Morehouse, the English preacher, says that when he was at home, in Manchester, in his boyhood, their family consisted of two brothers, two sisters, and the father—the mother having died. They were poor people, and his brother was a bad boy, a prodigal, and they could not get him to work in the mill.

One of the sisters said to her father: "Father, I will tell thee what thee ought to do with our John; turn him into the street."

"Why?" asked the father.

"Why," she said, "see how good we all are, and how bad he is; he is a disgrace to us. Turn him away."

Christmas Day came, and the family, including the wayward boy, were together. The old man read a chapter and prayed. Then, hoping the occasion would make her tender, he turned around to the daughter and said: "Well, what are we to do with thy brother now?"

But her heart was hard against him, she felt shamed and disgraced by him, and her reply was: "Put him in the street."

Then the old man turned to one of the friends who had been with them at their Christmas dinner, and put the question to him. He said he did not like to interfere, but he thought it might do him good to turn him out for a while. The old man left his chair, with the tears streaming down his face, and went across the room and put his arms around the bad boy's neck and said: "John, thy sister and brother and friend say I should turn thee out; but I am thy poor old father, and I will never put thee in the street, my boy."

The wicked son, who had stood out against everything else with hard heart, melted at the father's love. It was the means of his giving his heart to Christ, and he became a noble preacher of the Gospel.

Oh, all the world may turn against you, but God has commended his love to you in following you while you were a sinner; tho you have slighted him, and grieved him, and crucified Jesus Christ afresh, and put his name to an open shame, yet still he seeks after you to save you.

William Dawson, a Yorkshire farmer, who became a famous soul-winner, had often made the public declaration that there was no man so far gone in London that Christ would not receive him. One day a young lady called on him and said:

"I heard you say once that there was no man so far gone in London that Christ would not receive him. Did you mean it?"

"Yes," he said.

"Well," she said, "I have found a man who says he is so bad that the Lord will not have anything to do with him. Will you go and see him?"

He said: "I will be glad to go."

She took him to a brick building in a narrow street; the sick man was in the fifth story. She said: "You had better go in alone."

He found there in that lonely garret, on a heap of old straw, a man who was evidently very sick. Mr. Dawson spoke a few kind words to him, and wanted to know if he should not call his friends.

The dying man said: "You are mistaken in the person."

"Why so?"

"I have no friends on earth."

Ah, how the devil does deceive men. He tells a man that the way to be popular and have many friends is to be careless about God and righteousness, and not to be too conscientious; but if a man goes on serving him, the time comes when the friends disappear.

"Well," said Mr. Dawson, "you have a friend in Christ"; and he told him how Jesus loved and pitied him, and would save him. He read here and there a paragraph from this great treasury book of kindness and love which the Bible is, and then tenderly prayed with him.

As the good man prayed, the light of hope from

the Word of God began to break into his dark soul, and his heart went out toward those against whom he had so deeply sinned. He said: "If my father would only forgive me, I could die happy."

"Who is your father?"

He told him, and Mr. Dawson said: "I will go and see him."

"No," the sick man said, in despair; "he has cast me off."

But William Dawson was not the man to give up the trail when he had once got on the track of the possible salvation of a soul, and so he persisted and got the father's address, and said: "I will go."

He went to a fashionable part of the West End of London, and rang the bell of the mansion where the father lived. A servant in livery came to the door, and showed him into the parlor. In a few moments the merchant came in. Mr. Dawson said to him: "You have a son by the name of Joseph."

The merchant gave a start, and, flushing with anger, replied: "No, sir; if you have come to talk to me about that worthless vagabond, you shall leave the house. I have disinherited him."

Mr. Dawson said: "He will not be your boy by night; but he will be as long as he lives."

The proud man's face softened, and in a husky voice he said: "Is my boy sick?"

"Yes, he is dying. I do not ask you to help bury him. I will attend to that; but he wants you to forgive him, and then he will die in peace."

Ah, what a poor thing is all our pride, and all our show of self-will, when once the heart is touched! The tears trickled down the cheeks of the father who had been so angry only a moment ago, and he sobbed out: "Does Joseph want me to forgive him? I would have forgiven him long ago if I had known that."

In a few moments they were in a carriage. They went to the house where the boy was; and as they ascended the filthy stairs the father groaned: "Did you find my boy here? I would have taken him to my heart if I had known this."

The boy cried, when his father came in: "Can you forgive me all my past sins?"

The father bent over him, his tears falling like rain, and kissed him, and said: "I would have forgiven you long ago." And he added: "We must get you down-stairs into the carriage and take you home."

But the dying man shook his head. "I am too sick—I am near the end—but I can die happy now. I believe that God for Christ's sake has forgiven me."

The young man told the father of the Savior's

love; and then, his head lying upon his father's bosom, he breathed his last in peace.

If a proud, self-willed human father could forgive like that, how much more confidently you may come to the heavenly Father, the very essence of whose heart is love, and who is always seeking our good.

And yet it is not possible for even God to bring to us the comfort of forgiveness and salvation except as we repent of and confess our sins. I think the sweetest promise in all the Bible for most people is the one which says: "As one whom his mother comforteth, so will I comfort you." But a mother can not comfort, oftentimes, without repentance and confession. Here is a wide-awake, irrepressible, jolly boy of thirteen, whose mother discovers him in the dreariest corner of the most unfrequented spot about the grounds. The world is evidently very dark to the boy at the present moment. The forlorn, utterly miserable look on his face bears abundant witness to that. Suddenly the mother comes upon the lad.

"Frank, did you hurt Stella?" she questions.

"Yes; but, mother, I didn't mean to."

"Then come and tell her so."

"Oh, but, mother, I didn't mean to," remonstrates the boy.

"Then come and tell her so," the mother repeats, in a tone which the boy knows means just what it says. The mother is inexorable. Her love is too wise to allow anything else. Reluctantly the boy obeys. Five minutes later he is one of the gayest of the crowd. The forlorn, miserable feeling is all gone. His mother has effectually comforted him.

So, with all the tenderness of a mother-heart, God is seeking to comfort some of you who are here now; but unless you will break down your self-will before him, repent of your sins, and confess them, and confess Christ as your Savior, even the mother-heart of divine tenderness can not comfort you or save you.

ESCAPE FROM A FATAL HANDICAP.

"O wretched man that I am! Who shall deliver me out of the body of this death?"—*Rom.* vii. 24 (Rev. Ver.).

"There is therefore now no condemnation to them that are in Christ Jesus. For the law of the Spirit of life in Christ Jesus made me free from the law of sin and of death."—*Rom.* viii. 1, 2 (Rev. Ver.).

THESE are terribly earnest sentences uttered by an earnest man. There is always hope for a man who is in earnest. Christ felt in his day that there was much more hope for the publicans and harlots, the outbreaking, shameful sinners, than there was for the Pharisees and scribes, who had lost the energy of life and the earnestness out of their souls.

Nobody is in a greater danger of eternal overthrow and defeat than the man or woman who goes along the way of life living only in the present, indifferent and thoughtless about the things of the highest importance. The man who realizes that he is a sinner, who has struggled to get away from his sins and found them hanging like a burden on his back—a horrid burden that might be compared to a dead body, which he loathes, and from which he has no power in himself to escape—is in a hopeful condition, because you do not need to argue with him to convince him that he is a sinner; but the people who are in greatest danger are those whose sins seem to them only mistakes or blunders to be apologized for. When Paul came to see down into the depths of his heart, he called himself with all honesty the chief of sinners, tho he had kept the ten commandments, so far as they affected his outward conduct and morality, from his youth up, and says that touching the righteousness that is in the law he was blameless. Do not for a moment congratulate yourself that you are not a sinner against God and living daily under condemnation of the law of God, because your sins are not so outbreaking and disgraceful as those which are generally held up for rebuke. It is not the poisonous gas that smells the worst which is the most dangerous to human life. Sewer gas of the worst sort has no odor; and the most poisonous exhalations are only perceptible by their deadly effects.

Alexander Maclaren says that Paul thought himself the chief of sinners not because he had broken the commandments, but because through all the respectability and morality of his early life there ran this streak—an alienation of heart, in the pride of self-confidence, from God, and an ignorance of his own wretchedness and need. The deep universal sin does not lie in the indulgence of passions or the breach of moralities, but in living a life of indifference to God, refusing to the Christ who died to redeem you your open friendship and willing service. Tho you have kept every moral requirement from your birth until now, yet if the Scripture accusation is true concerning you, that "the God in whose hand thy breath is, and whose are all thy ways, thou hast not glorified," that is enough, if you could only see it in its true light, to brush away all the respectabilities and proprieties and worldly graces, and cause you, looking at the black reality of rebellion against the good God, to wail out: "O wretched man that I am, who shall deliver me out of the body of this death?"

The work of salvation is quick when you come to recognize your sins and break down your will in complete humility before the mercy-seat. A little boy had once been attending a revival meeting like this, and he went home to his mother one evening and said: "Mother, John Jones is under conviction and seeking for peace, but he will not find it to-night, mother."

"Why, William?" said she.

"Because he's only down on one knee, mother,

and he never will get peace until he is down on both knees."

That boy had found a vein of eternal truth. Salvation never can come to us without obedience to God. When we have lost faith in ourselves, have ceased to apologize for our sins, have given up all hope of a compromise, and have made an unconditional surrender of our hearts and our wills to Christ, then the deadly handicap of sin will be taken away. We have nothing at all to offer as merit for ourselves. A man who has nothing but a dead body tied on his back is not in a position to dictate terms. It is not justice he wants, but mercy.

In the days when the first Napoleon was all-powerful in France, a little girl of fourteen years came alone to the gate of the palace. Her tears and pleadings melted the heart of the porter, and he let her in. She went from one room to another, till she found her way to the hall through which she learned Napoleon and his officers were soon to pass. When he appeared, she threw herself at his feet, and with all her soul in her voice cried: "Pardon, sire! Pardon for my father!"

"What is your name?" inquired the emperor.

"My name is Lajolia," she said; and with flowing tears added, "but, sire, my father is doomed to die."

"Ah, young lady," replied Napoleon, "I can do nothing for you. It is the second time in which your father has been found guilty of treason against the state."

"Alas!" exclaimed the poor girl, "I know it, sire; but I do not ask for justice—I implore pardon. I beseech you, forgive, oh, forgive my father!"

Napoleon's lips trembled, and, hard as he often was, his eyes filled with tears. After a momentary struggle of feeling, he gently took the hand of the young girl, and said: "Well, my child, for your sake I will pardon your father."

So the only cry appropriate to the lips of a sinner against God is for mercy, for forgiveness.

I call your attention to the completeness, the abundance of salvation in Jesus Christ. When once a man surrenders his will to Christ, and lays down his body of death at the foot of the cross, he steps out into an experience where there is no condemnation, but a spirit of freedom and gladness. Christ is able to give us perfect release.

A little girl had once been frightened by hearing the talk of older people about the power and vicious spirit of Satan. On the first opportunity she said to her father: "Is Satan bigger than me?"

"Yes," replied her father.

"Is he bigger than you?"

"Ah, yes," was the sad reply.

"And is Satan bigger than Jesus Christ?"

"No."

"Well, then," said the little girl, brightening up, "I don't care a rap for him!"

Thank God! we may have the strength of Jesus Christ added to our own, and that will turn the saddest defeat into the most glorious victory. If we turn from our sins with repentance, abhorring them, and yield ourselves to be the willing friends of Christ, he will not only relieve us from the sins of the past, and from the wicked appetites, the unholy passions, and the spirit of rebellion against God, which are like a body of death, but with the most gracious love he will bestow upon us the honor of his own name, the badge of his affection.

When Napoleon III. was at the height of his career, he conceived the idea of bestowing the cross of the Legion of Honor upon Rosa Bonheur, the famous painter, but he was fearful that the popular judgment might condemn him for granting it to a woman. Finally he fell upon a happy expedient. Going from home for an excursion, he left his wife, the empress, as regent. From the imperial residence at Fontainebleau it was only a short distance to the little village of By, where the artist lived and worked. One day, entirely unannounced, the empress entered the studio where Rosa Bonheur was at work. She rose, abashed, to receive her distinguished visitor, who threw her arms about her neck and kissed her. The empress remained but a few moments, and it was not until after she had gone that the artist discovered that, as the royal visitor had given her the kiss, she had pinned upon her blouse the cross of the Legion of Honor!

So it is, broken down by sin, thinking most of the body of death from which he would escape, a poor sinner comes to Christ, and the Savior throws his arms about his neck, and not only his sins pass away, but in all the years to come he wears the badge of Christ's royal name, and is honored with communion and fellowship with him who is his King and his Lord.

Many of you who hear me know enough about Christ and about the Gospel to be saved, but you wait and wait, as tho you expected some flood of supernatural influence would rise about you and sweep you off your feet and carry you against your will into the kingdom of God. You may be very sure that such a thing will never happen. If it should it would do you no good, for it would not change your character. The first move must come from you. God has done everything he can do for your salvation, until you yourself act in obedience to him. The reason you do not move is because you are chained by your sins. You must break those chains so far as to accept Christ, or you will be lost forever. You are like boats that are fastened to the shore—there is no use pulling at the oars until the chain is unfastened. Some of you are like Herod, who was bound by his unholy lust for the wicked woman who lived with him, and tho the greatest preacher of repentance that ever lived thundered his warning in his ears, and wrought upon his judgment and emotion, he was left unsaved. Some of you are in lethargy. You are like ships becalmed at sea. You get nowhere. If you would only act, if you would only obey the Lord Jesus, the breeze of the Holy Spirit brought by that obedience would fill your sails and you would make progress toward the divine life.

A young man of northern New York was lost for two days and nights in the wilds of the Adirondacks. Just as the searchers and his family were ready to give him up as dead, he was found in a half-dazed condition. He had started out in the morning bear-hunting, expecting to return at night. When darkness fell he was many miles from home, weary, and faint with hunger. He made himself a bed of balsam boughs, and lay down and fell asleep beside a fire of pine knots. Long after midnight he was awakened by a strange sound. He leaped to his feet and caught up his gun. He saw a pair of yellow eyes peering at him from the shadows, and he raised his gun and fired. Having scared away the panther, he threw more pine knots on the fire and fell asleep again. When day dawned he awoke, chilled to the bone and very hungry. He wondered how far he was from home, and struck manfully out, soon leaving his camp far behind. About the middle of the afternoon he saw a thin column of smoke rising in the distance, from a clump of balsam firs. The sight enthused the lost boy. "I knew I'd run across some cabin if I kept going long enough," he said joyfully to himself. For an hour the boy walked with quickened pace. Then he came upon his camp of the night before. The dying fire was sending up a faint pencil of smoke. With despair he sank wearily down upon his couch of balsam boughs. He had done what many persons have done before him when lost in a wilderness—simply wandered about in a circle, eventually coming back to his starting-place.

The prospect of spending another night in the great woods positively appalled him. Slowly and painfully he struggled to his feet, gathered a fresh supply of pine knots, and threw some of them on the fire. He huddled close to the blazing knots, and tried to keep back the pangs of hunger that were driving him half mad.

The next morning he set out again. He staggered about the forest all day, until toward evening he sank down upon a big rock and gave himself up for lost. He was beginning to feel strangely faint. Suddenly the crack of a rifle pierced the stillness of the forest. He listened intently. The shot was repeated. Hope began to grow in his heart. Possibly that was a signal from somebody looking for him. He raised his own gun in the air and fired. Help was at hand, and in less than half an hour he was in the hands of his friends and his troubles were over.

Does not a good part of this story illustrate your experience? You have wandered away from God. You are lost in the mountains of sin. You have wandered about in your thinking on the subject, and have had many noble impulses, many longings to live a better life, but you have come back again to your old camp of inaction. Tho you have been often under conviction of sin, you have gone round and round in a circle and gotten nowhere, and have come no nearer to salvation by all your thinking.

My friends, we are searching for you in the name of Jesus Christ our Lord. We are a searching party under the direction of your Savior, and it is my gracious privilege, through God's mercy, to signal to you that help is at hand. Will you not signal us in return? That lost boy might have sat there on the rock in the forest until he starved to death, had he not signaled back to those that were searching for him to save him. So all heaven is searching for you. Christ has promised that, on the first signal from you, he will come to your relief. But you are a free moral agent, and he can not and will not break down your will. The first move now must come from you. The greatest tragedy of human life is that a man by his own inaction may make it impossible even for the Almighty God to save him. I appeal to you not so to sin against your own soul!

REAPING OUR OWN SOWING.

"Be not deceived; God is not mocked: for whatsoever a man soweth, that shall he also reap. For he that soweth unto his own flesh shall of the flesh reap corruption; but he that soweth unto the Spirit shall of the Spirit reap eternal life."—*Gal.* vi. 7, 8 (Rev. Ver.).

A MAN holds his destiny in his own hands just as surely as a farmer decides what his harvest shall be by the seed which he sows in the springtime. He who sows barley must not expect oats; he who scatters thistles must not look for wheat; if he does, he will be disappointed. Every intelligent farmer expects to reap what he sows. He knows that the quantity of the harvest will depend on some things that are beyond his control; the amount of rain and sunshine will have something to do with that. But whether the harvest be great or small, the quality of it he decides when, looking over his fields, he determines what shall be sown.

This analogy holds good in the spiritual world. A man can not sow vulgarity and expect to reap a pure mind. A man can not sow evil imaginings and reap noble conversation and conduct. He can not sow hardness of heart and reap a brotherly soul. He can not sow neglect and indifference of Christ and reap divine fellowship or a good conscience. The quantity of the harvest may vary according to a man's associations or gifts, which tend to develop one phase or another of his character, but the quality of the harvest every one of us absolutely controls by the seeds of thought and conduct which we are sowing in our own hearts or lives. Every one may rest assured that his eternal salvation hinges upon his own will. For whether we reap sorrow or joy, whether of the flesh we reap corruption or of the Spirit reap eternal life, it will not be our father's or mother's, it will not be our neighbor's, neither will it be God's harvest that we reap—every man must reap of his own sowing. God does not desire the death of any, but rather that all should turn and live. No man can say when he is tempted that it is of God, for God tempts no man to sin. There used to be a good deal of quibbling about the expressions in the Book of Exodus which state that God hardened the heart of Pharaoh. God did not harden the heart of Pharaoh except as he hardens the ripening kernel of wheat when it is exposed to the sun. Pharaoh had every opportunity of salvation. Moses came before him as the messenger of God, and demanded in the name of the Lord that he let Israel go, and Pharaoh's great sin was in that first refusal to the demand of God. That made easier his next refusal, and the next; and tho on the occasion of every plague that came upon him and his people he was convicted anew of his sin and disposed to relent, yet every time it became easier for him to harden his heart and refuse to surrender his will to God, because the restraints of the grace of God had less and less effect on him. Pharaoh sowed obstinate self-will and he reaped the same. When once that seed was in the soil, it took no special decree of God to harden his heart, as the farmer needs not to sow his field again after it is once rooted. The seed of rebellion which Pharaoh sowed when he first refused to yield to the Lord brought up a harvest after its own kind. And so the old Egyptian monarch went on from one degree of wicked obstinacy to another, till at last even the slaying of the first-born from the palace to the hovel throughout all the land of Egypt was not enough to break down his rebellious will, and he followed the children of God until the waves of the Red Sea swept above his hosts, a historical witness to all the generations to come of the truth of the statement that "whatsoever a man soweth that shall he also reap." God was just as good to Pharaoh as he will be to us.

He had a fair chance, and will never dare to stand up in the day of judgment, after all the warnings and rebukes and invitations which God sent to him, and say: "I did not have a fair chance." He will be compelled to wail: "My condemnation is just!"

This same hardening of heart is going on in some of you now. When you began to stifle its protests, you began to sow the smothering of conscience, and with some this has gone on until conscience has become very feeble. Every time you refuse to heed its remonstrance against wrong-doing, your power to stifle your conscience is increased manyfold, and so the harvest you reap is a smothered conscience. And if you continue, the time will come when conscience will become silent and you will go recklessly into sin without alarm, scarcely knowing that sin is sin—calling good evil, and evil good; but remember, if you sow a smothered conscience you will reap a remorse that all eternity will not be able to silence!

This sowing to the flesh referred to in the text means the sowing to your passions and your appetites, so that you indulge yourself in a sinful way. And what a man sows in that way he reaps, and the harvest is corruption. But let us understand that no soul is ever lost through any arbitrary decree of God. It is only that a man reaps his own sowing. You may illustrate this by any phase of your soul life. Suppose you are moved by the Holy Spirit to accept Christ as your Savior; you resist the call, and in order to do so effectually throw yourself into some giddy pleasure, or into irreligious associations, or, it may be, only immerse yourself the deeper into your studies or business, hoping thereby to rid yourself of the disturbing call of the Spirit of God. In doing that you have sown resistance to God's Spirit. Having refused the Holy Spirit once, it is easier for you to do so the second time, and easier the next, and the next, until you reap a harvest that finally grieves away the Spirit of God, and it can be said of you: "He is joined unto his idols, let him alone."

Again, suppose you are tempted to do something which you know is a sin against God. You yield to the temptation, tho the protest of your hitherto pure conscience makes it hard for you. That is a seed sown, and it is much easier to commit that sin again than if you had not yielded at first; and every time you yield another stone goes off the wall of your resistance, until after a while there is no wall left, and sinful indulgences troop into your heart and life over a dusty path worn deep by oft-repeated wickedness.

Take an illustration of another kind. You were

brought up to pray at your mother's knee, and perhaps when you came away from home she gave you a Bible and you promised to read a chapter every day and maintain your habits of worship; but you are in a hurry some day, and you omit your Bible reading. It troubles you all day and you say to yourself: "Mother's gentle heart would be grieved if she knew it. I'm sorry I didn't take the time, for her sake at least, to read it." You miss, too, the influence of that pure glimpse into the spiritual value of things which your Bible reading has heretofore given you to look at and study at moments of ease during the day. That omission is a seed. The next time you are in a hurry and fail to read your chapter, you think less about it, and so you go on until the harvest is that your Bible goes to the bottom of your trunk or to the topmost shelf of your bookcase. Having left off your Bible reading, it is easy to omit the prayer; and prayer omitted a few times reaps a harvest of worldliness, until the result is that you are coming to live as tho there were no God to whom you can pray, as tho there were no Bible with its inspiration for youth, with its comfort for sorrow, with its pillow of promise for the dying, with its Christ and forgiveness for the sinner, and its hope of eternal life. And so, through the whole history of a man's life, if he shall reject

God and yield himself to sin, it is harvest after harvest until the great harvest of punishment at last is only that a man is filled with his own way and permitted to reap his own sowing.

This makes the Bible warnings of a coming punishment for sin very simple and natural, but very terrible. Hardened sinners have been wont to sneer and scoff at the words of Christ which describe the final estate of the impenitent soul as "the outer darkness" where there is "gnashing of teeth," or picture the thirsty soul in a gulf of fire crying for "a drop of water" to cool his tongue, or portray the fire that never can be quenched and the gnawing worm that never dies; but I am sure that all these illustrations taken together are not so terrible as this simple statement that a sinful soul, a wicked life, shall reap its own sowing and feed upon it forever. All you have to do is to let this wickedness go on; let a man reap what he has sown in sin, and there is a harvest of remorse forever to be gathered. A man "sows to the flesh," says Paul, and "of the flesh he reaps corruption." That is, a man tampers with and fattens and feeds the sinful lusts of his body—these are seeds he sows; they have their wicked counterpart in his mind, in his imagination. These lusts and appetites and passions bear harvest, and they come back on the man who sowed them with cravings and gnawings that demand of him ever fresh gratification. Now the solemn word of Christ is that a man will be in the next world just what he is here, except that there he will not have the chance to repent and change, but must go on reaping what he has sown here. Can you think of a more terrible punishment than that? Here is a drunkard who has sown an appetite for strong drink, and he has gathered his harvest and sown it again until even in this world he has come to the place where he reaps a harvest of agony untold. Can you imagine a more terrible hell than that a man shall go on reaping a harvest like that? Forever thirsting for strong drink, its tiger-like fierceness forever craving, and yet never satisfied? Before such a picture Dives in hell longing for a drop of water to cool his tongue seems tame. And so you may go on through the whole list. Let the envious man just keep his envy and be shut up to live with it forever—his envy always burning all peace out of his heart. Let the jealous man be forever jealous. Let the revengeful soul harbor his malice, nursing it to keep it warm, seeking for a chance to get his revenge upon his victim. Let the lustful soul be forever planning and scheming for the gratification of unholy passion. Let the victim of greed, with the money-fever in his blood, never lose the heat out of his veins that makes him cry out constantly for more, and more, and yet never attain his desired end. That is, let every sinner reap his own sowing—and you have a fire in each soul that never will be quenched; you have an undying worm gnawing its agonizing way, that never ends, through the quivering heart-strings. God save a man from a doom like that!

And, thank God! that is what he wants to do! For Jesus Christ came to save sinners—not save you *in* your sins, but to save you *from* your sins. It is God's desire that the Holy Spirit shall plow your heart for a new sowing; that the old growths of sin and wickedness shall be uprooted—not chopped down, with the roots remaining in the soil of your soul, but dug out—so that your heart may be tilled like a garden; and the heavenly Gardener will sow in that clean heart, in that renewed spirit, the seeds of love, and hope, and faith, and meekness, and gentleness, and reverence, and patience, until your soul shall become a flower garden, fragrant with the graces of Christian life.

Blessed be God, goodness is as contagious as badness! The seeds of righteousness will bear as abundant a harvest as the seeds of evil. If you will sow now the seed of repentance and faith, you shall grow a harvest of tenderness of heart, of confidence in God, of love for your brother, and of joy of soul; and as the seeds of goodness are sown in your heart, gracious harvests shall wave there that will not only make your own life glad and peaceful, but make you a great blessing to all who come in contact with you.

As these meetings have gone on, and you have listened to the joyous testimonies of some of these saintly men and women, the fragrance of whose lives is "like ointment poured forth," I know you have said to yourself: "When I get to be an old man or an old woman, and my hair is white, and eternity can not be far off, I want to be a man or a woman like that." Then, I beg you, sow the same kind of seed. Such a harvest of noble manhood and holy womanhood does not come by accident. Behind these ripening shocks is more than half a century of devout Christian experience. They gave their hearts to God in youth. All their lives they have been sowing the seeds of faith, and hope, and love, and obedience—and the result is the harvest which it so delights you to behold. If you want to be good old men and lovable and happy old women, you must prepare for such a harvest. Begin here and now by yielding your hearts to the Christ who has been and is their Savior and Lord.

DESTINY DECIDED IN YOUTHFUL DAYS.

"Having been reminded of the unfeigned faith that is in thee; which dwelt first in thy grandmother Lois, and thy mother Eunice; and, I am persuaded, in thee also."— 2 *Tim.* i. 5 (Rev. Ver.).

PAUL gives us here a glimpse into the background of Timothy's life. The background of a great picture is often important. It is the womb of mystery out of which the deeds portrayed on the canvas have come. Every splendid deed, every noble man, every holy woman have behind them a background of hereditary influence which is always interesting. If I were a great painter, there is one picture I would like to paint as my contribution to religious art. It would be the picture of Kensington Common, with a crowd of twenty thousand people gathered to hear John Wesley, the mightiest religious leader of his century. I would paint the people by scores and hundreds on their knees in long rows, like a swath of grain fallen before the reaper, crying out to God for mercy and salvation under the spell of Wesley's burning words. Yet it is not Wesley, nor the great audience, nor the repenting sinners, upon whom I would concentrate the interest in the picture, but on the figure of an old woman standing behind the speaker, with hair as white as snow; a shining face, and eyes that pierce the veil of the eternities—the face of the prophetess she was—Susannah, the mother of the Wesleys.

Everything that John Wesley ever was, humanly speaking, he owed to his mother. The father was dreamy and poetical, but never able to make a living. Susannah Wesley was both father and mother, teacher and priestess, to a family of nineteen children. John was a dull lad at first, and did not learn easily. He had the same kind of traits that many boys have—he could forget knowledge more rapidly than he could acquire it. She taught him the alphabet twenty times, that, to use her own language, "the nineteenth might not be in vain."

Many a strong man who has done or is doing great work for humanity owes his power to the influence of some gentle mother whose name has never been known beyond the little community where she lived. Once when Daniel Webster, at the height of his fame, had been given a great reception in Boston, where the rich and great had been proud to do him homage and many an elegant lady had thrown bouquets of rarest flowers at his feet, as he turned to retire into his hotel a timid little girl paused before him and placed a bunch of old-fashioned garden pinks in his hand. At sight of these familiar flowers, and as their well-remembered fragrance filled the air, the old memories were stirred. Just such pinks used to grow in his mother's garden when he was a child. Instantly that sweet face of the loved mother came to his vision; her tender, gentle voice sounded once more in his ears. So overcome was he by the tide of memories which crowded into his heart, that he excused himself and went to his apartments alone. "Nothing in all my life," said he, "affected me like that little incident." Mary Clemmer had in her thought some circumstance like that when she sang:

> "From out the great world's rush and din
>   There came a guest;
> The inner court he entered in,
>   And sat at rest.
>
> "Slow on the wild tide of affairs
>   The gates were closed;
> Afar the hungry host of cares
>   At last reposed.
>
> "Then through the dim doors of the past,
>   All pure of blame,
> Came boyish memories floating fast—
>   His mother's name.

DESTINY DECIDED IN YOUTHFUL DAYS. 321

"'Ah! all this loud world calls the best
 I'd give,' he said,
'To feel her hand, on her dear breast
 To lean my head.

"'I cry within the crownèd day,
 That would be joy,
Could she but bear me far away,
 Once more her boy.'

. . . .

"Far out amid the earth's turmoils
 A strong man stands,
Upheld in triumph and in toils
 By unseen hands.

"But who may lift with subtle was
 The masks we wear?
I only know his mother's hand
 Is on his hair.

"I only know through all life's harms,
 Through sin's alloy,
Somehow, somewhere that mother's arms
 Will reach her boy."

No one can exaggerate the power of home influence. To be born in a Christian home and to grow to manhood or womanhood in the midst of prayer and song and reverent love, is the sweetest gift God can bestow upon youth. Sir Walter Scott had his favorite seat in his garden put within earshot of his bailiff's cottage, because it was a devout Christian family and he delighted to hear the sound when they sang the Psalms at morning and evening worship. There never was sweeter incense in this world than that which goes up in the home where parents and children together humbly and simply worship God. The hymns and Scripture learned in the home, and, above all, the confidence in God and the courage of the Christian faith that goes with it, will abide in the heart to rise again, even after years of wickedness, and make themselves felt as powerful factors in the life of those who have shared it.

A very graphic and beautiful illustration of this vitality of youthful teachings is found in S. R. Crockett's book, "The Men of the Moss Hags," in the account given of the little ones who were saved by the "Mother's Psalm." It was in a cruel and bloody time, and the hard soldiers of Westerha' had come upon a band of children, and the little cluster of Scotch bairns huddled together in fear. The cruel commander ordered them to kneel down to be shot, because the brave little souls would not tell where their fathers were hid. And then to taunt them, the cruel man cried out to them, "Bonny whigs ye air, to die without even a prayer. Put up a prayer this minute, for ye shall all die, every one of you."

And a little boy made answer to him: "Sir, we can not pray, for we be too young to pray."

"You are not too young to rebel, nor yet to die for it," was the brute-beast's reply.

Then with that, a little girl held up her hand as if she were answering a teacher in a class. "An' if it please ye, sir," she said, "me and Alec canna pray, but we can sing, 'The Lord's my Shepherd,' gin that will do. My mother learned it us afore she gaed awa'." And before any one could stop her she stood up like one that leads the singing in a kirk.

"Stand up, Alec, my wee mannie," she said.

Then all the bairns stood up. A hard soldier looking on declared it reminded him of Bethlehem and the night when Herod's troopers rode down to look for Mary's bonny Bairn. Then from the lips of babes and sucklings arose the quavering strains:

> "The Lord's my Shepherd, I'll not want.
>   He makes me down to lie
> In pastures green; He leadeth me
> The quiet waters by."

As they sang one of the troopers took out his pistols and began to sort and prime them, resolved to shoot down the leader of the band rather than see the little ones die with that Psalm on their lips. But there was no need, for as they sang he saw trooper after trooper turn away his head, for being Scottish bairns they had all learned that

Psalm. The ranks shook. Man after man fell out, and he saw the tears dropping down their cheeks. Finally one of the hardest men among all the persecutors broke down.

"Curse it, Westerha'," he cried, "I canna thole this langer."

And at last, even Westerha' turned his bridle rein and rode away from off the bonnie holms of Shield hill, for the victory was to the bairns. And the trooper wondered what the thoughts of his chief were; for he, too, had learned that Psalm at the knees of his mother. And as the troopers rode loosely up hill and down brae, broken and ashamed, the sound of those bairns' singing followed after them, and soughing across the fells came the words:

> "Yea, tho I walk in Death's dark vale,
>   Yet will I fear none ill:
> For thou art with me; and thy rod
>   And staff me comfort still."

Then Westerha' swore a great oath, and put spurs in his horse, to get clear of the sweet singing that was like the dagger of avenging justice in his heart.

In this long campaign for souls which we have had together, nothing has pleased me more than the family altars which have been erected, and the husbands and wives who have been united in the service of the Lord, and are henceforth to join in a fellowship of worship and be united in their efforts to bring up their children to be, like Timothy, grounded in the faith of the Gospel. Many times it happens that a wife is left to bear alone all the burden of the instruction and training of the children in a religious way. I am sure there are some manly men who remain out of the church and let their wives go on carrying this double burden, who would take a different attitude if they could only clearly see how utterly unworthy of them is such a position. A sensible and intelligent man of the world was heard not long ago to make this statement concerning his wife, who had just given her heart to God and was seeking to bring the spirit of Christianity into her home: "My wife is a professor of religion, and I am standing off to see what good it is going to do her." Could there be anything more mean and cowardly, more unmanly, than that? As the man remarked who overheard it, if his wife were rowing a boat against a stiff current, and her life and the fate of his children depended on the result, he would not count it either wise or manly for him to sit on the bank of the stream and coolly pass judgment on the skill of her strokes. And yet, my brother, is that not what you are doing if, while your wife is earnestly seeking to be a Christian, you refuse to give her your fellowship and sympathy, but view the church and her efforts with a critical eye? There are parents in this presence who are not Christians. You are throwing the silent influence of your daily life against Christ, and against the church, and setting an example of indifference to Christianity before your children, thus robbing them of the sweetest memories they ought to have—memories of faith and hope and prayer that would hallow and make sacred their childish days.

Give your hearts to God now! Make the Bible the book of counsel in your home. Bring reverence and worship to your fireside, and your children will rise up to call you blessed in all the years to come.

THE GREATEST SAYING IN THE WORLD.

"Faithful is the saying, and worthy of all acceptation, that Christ Jesus came into the world to save sinners."—1 *Tim.* i. 15 (Rev. Ver.).

THE most important embassy that was ever sent in connection with the history of this world was the embassy of Jesus Christ from the court of heaven to the men and women of earth. He came from God to save us from our greatest trouble, which is our sin. We may know what Jesus Christ thinks of sin by the prophecy of Isaiah which he applied to himself in his first sermon at Nazareth: "The spirit of the Lord God is upon me; because the Lord hath anointed me to preach good tidings unto the meek; he hath sent me to bind up the broken-hearted, to proclaim liberty to the captives, and the opening of the prison to them that are bound; to proclaim the acceptable year of the Lord, and the day of vengeance of our God; to comfort all that mourn; to appoint unto them that mourn in Zion, to give unto them a garland for ashes, the oil of joy for mourning, the garment of praise for the spirit of heaviness." And when the disciples of John the Baptist went to him from John's prison, desiring to know if he was indeed the Messiah or whether they should look for another, Jesus told them to go back to John in prison and give him his credentials. He said to them: "Tell John the things which ye do hear and see: the blind receive their sight, and the lame walk, the lepers are cleansed, and the deaf hear, and the dead are raised up, and the poor have good tidings preached to them."

From these statements we know that Jesus Christ came to save sinners, because sin was marring and destroying humanity as nothing else can. To his thought sin makes men poor. It takes from them the highest and noblest riches. It does not matter how many corner lots a man may own, or how large his bank account may be, if he has lost his peace with God, has laid up no treasures in heaven, and possesses no title to an inheritance in the life beyond, he is a poor man. Men may call him rich, as did the neighbors in the Gospel story of the old farmer, who had planned to pull down his barns and build greater and congratulate his soul upon the increase of his wealth. Men called him a rich man, but God called him a "fool"; and so, no matter how much wealth you have in this world, if you have no treasure in heaven, if you are a sinner against God—then, being only a tenant at the will of God in the things you have here, you are likely to be a pauper before to-morrow morning. They may bury you in a better coffin than they would ordinary paupers, but there will be no bank book in the pockets of your burial suit. Often when I stand at a funeral and look down on the body of a man dressed in his best clothes, I reflect that all his life long he has been careful when he went on a journey to have plenty of money in his pocket, and, if it were a long journey across the sea, a letter of credit; and now, for the first time, he is going on a long journey with empty pockets. It is a very little nook of our lives in which earthly wealth is of any value. In the long eternal life only spiritual wealth counts, and that is where sin makes men poor. I have read of a band of thieves who lay in ambush for some miners who were coming home from the gold-fields, bringing their bags of dust and their nuggets to market. And the thieves emptied the sacks of the gold and filled them up with worthless sand. Ah, that is what sin does for its victims! It takes away a man's innocency, his reverence, his worshipful spirit, his trust in God, his faith in Jesus Christ, his title to heaven, and gives him in exchange bags of sand which have no purchasing power in the land to which he is going. No wonder Isaiah asks: "Wherefore do ye spend money for that which is not bread? and your labor for that which satisfieth not?"

Not only does sin make men poor, but it makes them prisoners. The captives of sin are upon every side of us. Look where we will and we behold men and women who are held in awful bondage by wicked habits. Men have said to me: "I would gladly be a Christian, but I am so wicked, my habits are so fastened on me, and I am so placed, that it would only be failure. I dare not make the attempt." Think of a man such a slave that he dare not even attempt to escape from his prison! Oh, the prisoners of sin who are in this city! Men held by chains of drink—yes, and women, too, until the love of motherhood is lost out of the soul! Souls held by chains of lust as black as Herod's, until their prison walls shut out the sunlight of hope, and dreams of escape are a thing of the past. Men bound by handcuffs of selfishness, and greed, and jealousy, and envy, and revenge; who seek to break away again and again and fall back only the more hopeless captives of their sins. Ah, yes, not a man here will deny that sin makes prisoners of its victims.

Sin breaks hearts. Every newspaper is full of the records of the broken hearts of the world. In their stories of divorce, and strife, and murder, and suicide, the daily newspapers present an awful picture of the broken hearts whose miseries have come from sin; and yet what they show us, compared to the great seething torrent of human agony rising from breaking hearts that is covered up and never comes to the public eye, is like Niagara's spray to its waters. Sin has broken the heart of mankind, and all about us men and women are walking with coffins in their breasts, wherein are buried their most sacred hopes. Ah, yes; sin breaks the heart!

I can not now tell you how sin makes men blind as to who their tyrant is, so that they hug their chains instead of turning from them with eager hearts to welcome the Deliverer.

It was because of this horrid havoc of sin in the world, wasting and desolating the hearts of men, that Jesus Christ, leaving all the glory of heaven, came down to earth to save sinners. Thank God, the saying is faithful! Jesus not only came to save sinners, but he has been saving them ever since he came. He saved Paul, blasphemer, persecutor, and Pharisee tho he was, and Paul declares that in saving him he saved "the chief of sinners"; for sin had so blinded him that he called evil good, and good evil, and boasted that he was doing the will of God when he was persecuting the disciples of Jesus to the very death; yet he who came to save sinners saved him. He can save any man who will come unto him in humility and faith. The conditions are very simple—only to turn away from the sin that despoils you and accept of the salvation which he died to purchase in your behalf.

Simply being sorry for our sins is no acceptance of salvation. We must be sorry in the same way as was the prodigal in Christ's story. He did not come home saying to his father, "I am hungry and ragged and dirty." The burden of his cry was: "I have sinned, and am unworthy." That is a plea that never will go unheeded in the ear of God. There is no virtue in being sorry for your sins; the most wicked-hearted man in the world is sorry for his sin when he has been lassoed by the law and held for punishment. But real repentance is a sorrow for sin that turns a man's feet from its path, and leads him to the mercy-seat, where with humble heart he confesses his transgressions and pleads for forgiveness in Jesus's name.

The Christ who came to save sinners saves them in the most gracious and loving way. Among the Orientals, when a man's debt has been paid either by himself or his friend, or when his creditor has taken pity on him because of his misfortune or his poverty and forgiven him the debt, it is the custom for the creditor to visit the house of the man who has owed him and nail the canceled bond over the door of the debtor, that everybody who passes by may see that the debt is paid. So when we repent of our sins and accept the salvation of Jesus Christ he pays our debts for us. Indeed, he has paid our debt already, but the canceled bond can never be nailed above our door until we accept it.

I do not want you to fail to see that pivotal point in our text—"worthy of all *acceptation.*" That the statement that Christ came to save sinners, and is saving sinners, is *worthy*, you all know. Day after day, for the past month, here at this altar men and women and boys and girls, all ages and conditions in life, have heard the message of salvation, and on accepting it have found it true. They declare that the half was never told them of the goodness of Christ. They bear testimony that their sins are forgiven; that instead of a rebuking, stinging conscience, they now have peace with God that casts out all fear. It is a worthy saying. The one thing that remains is, "*Have you accepted it?*" Not, Do you believe it theoretically? Not, Are you an admirer of Christian civilization and in sympathy with Christianity in a dreamy sort of way? Neither, Have you accepted it so far that you expect some time in the future to avail yourself of the offer of mercy? I do not mean that.

Have you *accepted* it? Suppose you are a young man and out of a position, and you have gone, day after day, seeking work and finding none. Little by little all the means that you had laid by are spent, and one after another you have pawned the things that you could spare until your overcoat is at the pawnbroker's, and you are down to the last point of being turned into the street. And as you go shivering about in a hopeless way, seeking to find a place where you may earn your bread, you meet a man who is well known in the community as an employer. You have known a great many others to be employed by him. They all report that he pays good wages, and that he is so kind and generous that it is a joy and a delight to be in his service. And this man, so tried and trusted, offers you a good place. He says: "I do not know whether there will be any opening to-morrow or not, but to-day you can go to work; and if you go to work to-day, and are faithful, you can stay as long as you live. I never turn off any of my hands. I will pay you when you are sick just the same as when you are well, and I will take care of you when you are old, but I want you now. To-morrow may be too late. There have been many that thought well about entering my employ and I have urged upon them to begin at once, but they put it off and died in poverty." Well, you listen to all this, but some strange and awful stupor holds you back, and you come to your landlord who has given you notice that you must go into the street in a week's time, and when he urges you to pay him you say: "Oh, don't bother about it. I have just met the best employer in the city and he has offered me a place at good wages; your bill will be all right." And the landlord says, "Did you accept it?" and you reply: "Well, no; I was tempted to, but I thought I would take my chances till to-morrow or the next day, or next week. I will see him again." Ah, you can not imagine yourself in such folly as that in the matters of every-day life, and yet that little allegory is a faint type of your folly when you neglect the salvation offered by him who came down from heaven to save sinners, and who does save every sinner that yields his heart to him. Christ has been saving your neighbors and acquaintances, and offers to save you, here and now, and yet you delay to accept him. Others have delayed, and have died in the agonies of remorse, and yet when I urge upon you that "*to-day* is the day of salvation," and beg you to harden not your heart, you shrug your shoulders and say with a folly that is indescribable, "There's time enough yet!"

There is nothing in this world that would add to your happiness so much as to be rid of your sins.

Some of you think if you could have more money, a wider circle of friends, higher success in business, a better position in society, you would be a great deal happier than you are. You are failing to take into account that happiness is born of character and conduct, and not of circumstances. A pure soul and a useful life will always find happiness. An impure soul and a useless life is as prone to misery as the sparks are to fly upward. It is often not a change of circumstances that men need so much as a change of heart, a transformed nature. There has been a good deal in the newspapers recently concerning a poor fellow known as the "Millionaire Tramp." He died the other day in the greatest wretchedness. He never was a millionaire, but after being a beggar for thirty years he suddenly inherited fifteen thousand dollars. If he could have gotten with that a clean heart and self-respect and good habits, he might have found peace and usefulness in the closing days of his life. But fifteen thousand dollars in a man's pocket has no power to take lusts and passions and wicked appetites out of his heart. From being a tramp without money he came to be a tramp with money. His old habits clung to him. He still went around the country in his rags, wasting his money in riotous living like the prodigal of old, squandering it on his sins until it was all gone and he died the poor miserable pauper he had been for so long. He who above all others can come into your life and sweeten it, and enrich you with the noblest treasures, is Jesus Christ, who came into this world to save sinners. Give him the privilege of saving you now!

THE WAITING CROWNS.

"The time of my departure is come. I have fought the good fight, I have finished the course, I have kept the faith: henceforth there is laid up for me the crown of righteousness, which the Lord, the righteous judge, shall give to me at that day: and not only to me, but also to all them that have loved his appearing."—2 *Tim.* iv. 6-8 (Rev. Ver.).

NOTHING could show more clearly the earnest way in which Paul looked at life than the three figures which he uses here to describe his own career. "I have fought the good fight." Life to him was a battle. This was a favorite illustration with him. In another place he urges Timothy to equip himself to be "a good soldier of Jesus Christ." In Ephesians he points out the sort of an armor a man ought to have in order to make a successful fight against the sins and enemies which he must meet in the course of a human career. "Put on," says this veteran soldier of life, "the whole armor of God, that ye may be able to stand against the wiles of the devil. For our wrestling is not against flesh and blood, but against the principalities, against the powers, against the world-rulers of this darkness, against the spiritual hosts of wickedness in the heavenly places. Wherefore take up the whole armor of God, that ye may be able to withstand in the evil day, and, having done all, to stand. Stand therefore, having girded your loins with truth, and having put on the breastplate of righteousness, and having shod your feet with the preparation of the gospel of peace; withal taking up the shield of faith, wherewith ye shall be able to quench all the fiery darts of the evil one. And take the helmet of salvation, and the sword of the Spirit, which is the word of God: with all prayer and supplication, praying at all seasons in the Spirit."

Paul was not deceived. Life is a battle, and every one of you will find it so; and the reason we see about us so many discouraged, defeated men and women from whom all life's hopes seem to have vanished, whose golden age is all in the past, who have no future to which they look forward with joy, who have no courage with which to wrest victory out of defeat, is because they have gone out to the battle of life empty-handed, and have grappled with sin without an armor and without a sword.

Again Paul looks back over his life and says, "I have finished the course." Life is like a racecourse. Every man and woman born into the world is entered in the race. To achieve success in running a race one must not carry any baggage that impedes him. You never saw a man running a race handicapped with a valise, or with a big bundle on his back. He strips for the race; every muscle must be free; neither limbs nor body must be constrained. So Paul urges in his letter to the Hebrews: "Let us also, seeing we are compassed about with so great a cloud of witnesses, lay aside every weight, and the sin which doth so easily beset us, and let us run with patience the race that is set before us, looking unto Jesus." The reason you have fallen behind in your race toward heaven so that some of you feel that heaven is farther away than it was five or ten or twenty years ago, when you left home, is because you have been weighed down by sin, and you will have to cut loose the burdens of your sins or be eternally distanced.

Life is a serious trust in Paul's thought. "I have kept the faith." How is it with you? When you were a little child it was as easy and natural for you to believe in God, and in Christ, and in heaven, as it was to believe in your father and mother. It was as natural for you to pray as it was to talk to your mother. The Bible was the book of God's love to you. What have you done with that childish innocency and trust? What have you done with that simple faith in God and in his Book? That was a sacred trust committed to you. It ought to have grown with every year of your life, as, like Enoch of old, you walked with God and came to know him as the friend who stood by you in time of storms, a friend closer than a brother in the hours of sorrow, and your inspiration for every noble deed. Have you frittered it away? These are solemn questions. How goes the battle? How speeds your soul on the heavenly race? Are you keeping the trust God committed to you, so that you can meet him in the judgment with peace?

I am impressed with this Scripture in its suggestion that everything must be judged by what will be its result *at the end*. Paul is talking about a Christian life at the close of the earthly career. He is ready to sail now; the ship is in the dock, and the last rope is about to be thrown off, and the time of his *departure* is at hand. What a tone of victory there is about that very word "departure"! That is not the word of a defeated man, it is the cry of a victor; a prisoner or a slave never could use that word. Death is robbed of all its sting, and a knightly traveler who is at home in all the worlds of God is about to take his departure from a world where he has fought a good fight, run an honorable course, kept faithfully every trust committed to him. Covered with honors, he is going home to heaven to **wear** his crown.

I repeat, you must judge everything by the end. Sin often begins with pleasure, but it ends in bitter dregs. See the young man that gloats over his first gold. He says: "I've no time for religion, but I must make money"; and he goes into it with keen zest, and says, as he rubs his hands together over some sharp trade: "This is the life to live! I pity those poor superstitious fellows that feel that they've got to give up their Sundays to go to church, and a night or two every week to prayer-meetings, and give their money to benevolences and missions. Poor fellows, they're to be pitied!" But just wait until you see a poor old miser coming toward the end, with nobody to love him because he has never loved anybody. All his life he has been cultivating suspicions in his soul, and now he trusts nobody and thinks everybody wants to rob him; and with all generous blood frozen in his veins he comes to the last a pitiful, lonely creature. Or see the young pleasure-seeker who says: "I must sow my wild oats and have my good time. I can't afford to be a total abstainer when it adds so much to jollity to have a glass of wine, or a mug of beer, with the fellows." Yes, that is the beginning, but what about the end? Come with me to the cheap lodging-houses, notice the street corners and the low saloons. In an hour's walk you may see a thousand men who began just like that—with youth, a good name, strong health, good clothes, money in their pockets and good positions; but I'll show you those men to-night, ragged and haggard and nervous and seamed with sin, hopeless, and despairing. It was the froth they were drinking in their youth; they are drinking the dregs now. Well does God's Word declare that there is a way that seemeth right unto a man, but the end is death.

Down on the Gulf of Mexico, near the mouth of a little creek called the Blind Oso, lies a pile of human bones, the skeletons of more than half a hundred men, and this is their story: Long ago, more than a hundred years, a pirate ship had a habit of coming into the harbor there, and sending out its band of raiders through all the ranches round about, who in their lawlessness raided and plundered as they would. They grew bolder with their success, and finally, knowing that they were coming in at a certain time, a rancher gathered a great band of men to lie in ambush and await their landing. Sure enough, one day the pirate ship was seen approaching the mouth of the Blind Oso. After a time the boats were lowered, and a large party of the pirates came rowing leisurely toward shore. Their firearms were stacked in the bottom of the boats, and they seemed to have lost all fear of enemies on shore. The boats were pulled up to the bank, and the pirates stepped out and came clambering up just opposite where their enemies waited. As they were almost past the order to fire was given, and then a charge was made on the outlaws. The pirates had no chance to defend themselves, and every man of them was killed in a few minutes. Their bodies were not buried, but were piled up on the sand and made a feast for the carrion birds and hungry wolves for many days thereafter. The Mexicans of that region always shun the spot, and through all the years the bones have bleached in the Southern sun.

The presumptuousness of sin is like that. A man goes on raids of self-indulgence; he presumes on God's mercy not to smite him down in his sins. He may go unwhipped of justice for a time, but the end is the pile of bleaching bones on the sand, and it is as sure in this city as on the shores of the Gulf of Mexico. It is never safe to break the law of God, and every hour a man remains in sin he is guilty of the wildest folly and presumption. No wise man will ever attempt any deed on which God's law frowns. If you can not do what you are tempted to do without feeling the condemnation of God's law hanging over you, then be sure that danger and death lurk in the deed. There used to be legends of demon-prepared banquets which were spread in the desert to tempt some brave and noble knight from an honorable mission, and when the name of God was pronounced over these tempting feasts they vanished, and instead of a luxurious table with gold dishes filled with rarest dainties to tempt the appetite, there remained only a heap of dry sticks and stones on the sand. So unless you can pray God's blessing on your deed, and thus look forward to the final results of it with peace, you may be sure that it is a devil's fraud.

I am impressed, also, with the marvelous love of Jesus Christ, who comes down from heaven and bears our sorrow and shame, and dies on the cross, to lift the poor victims of sin out of their bondage and their trouble and make them the kind of men and women who shall be crowned in heaven. There is nothing that will adequately illustrate this love of God in Christ Jesus for condemned sinners.

When Madame Sontag began her musical career, it is said that she was brought into sharp rivalry with Amelia Steininger, who had already begun to decline because of dissipation. Once when Madame Sontag appeared in Vienna, the friends of her rival hissed her, causing her great annoyance and sorrow; but the years passed away, and later, when Madame Sontag was at the height of her fame, she was riding through the streets of Berlin and saw a little girl leading a blind woman. The queen of song stopped her carriage and said: "Come here, my little child, come here. Who is that you are leading by the hand?" And the wondering child replied: "That's my mother; that's Amelia Steininger. She used to be a great singer; but she lost her voice, and cried so much about it that she lost her eyesight."

"Give my love to her," said Madame Sontag, "and tell her an old acquaintance will call on her this afternoon."

The next week in Berlin a vast assemblage gathered at a benefit for that poor blind woman, and the people who listened thought Madame Sontag had never sung so like an angel before, and we may well believe it. And the generous woman employed a skilled oculist, who tried in vain to give sight again to her poor enemy. Until the day of Amelia Steininger's death, Madame Sontag tenderly cared for her, and befriended her daughter afterward.

What a glorious thing for a queen of song to do for one who had been her enemy! But I know a more wonderful story still! And there are multitudes here who would gladly testify to it. Here is a man who had sin and worldliness tempting him on one side, and the Christ who died to redeem him singing the heavenly song in his ears on the other, and in his blindness and hardness of heart he hissed the Lord away and went with his Lord's enemy; and yet Christ in infinite generosity and tenderness came back again and again and knocked at the door of his heart, until, at last, he was let in, and brought sight to the blind, bread to the hungry, the water of life to the thirsty, and led the enraptured soul upward to its crowning.

It was not only Paul who had such a glorious outlook for the future. Every Christian from that day till this who has served the Lord with gladness has come to the time of departure in peace. A good old Scotchman was dying on a Sunday night. The bell of the kirk was ringing, calling the people to church. The old saint heard it, and, half dreaming, thought he was on his way to the church as he used to be when he had to ford the river; and as the evening bell struck up he said: "Hark, children, the bells are ringing; we shall be late; we must make the mare step out quick!" He shivered and then said: "Pull the robe up closer, my lass! it is cold crossing the river, but we shall soon be there!" And he smiled and said: "Just there now." The sweetest smile that ever came upon the old grizzled face shone upon it then, for he had got to church—not to the old Highland kirk, but to the temple of the glorified.

Books by ❧ ❧

DR. LOUIS ALBERT BANKS.

Christ and His Friends.

A Collection of Revival Sermons, Simple and Direct, and Wholly Devoid of Oratorical Artifice, but Rich in Natural Eloquence, and Burning with Spiritual Fervor. The author has strengthened and enlivened them with many illustrations and anecdotes. 12mo, Cloth, Gilt Top, Rough Edges. Price, $1.50; post-free.

National Presbyterian, Indianapolis: "One of the most marked revivals attended their delivery, resulting in hundreds of conversions. Free from extravagance and fantasticism, in good taste, dwelling upon the essentials of religious faith, their power has not been lost in transference to the printed page."

New York Observer: "These sermons are mainly hortatory . . . always aiming at conviction or conversion. They abound in fresh and forcible illustrations. . . . They furnish a fine specimen of the best way to reach the popular ear, and may be commended as putting the claims of the Gospel upon men's attention in a very direct and striking manner. No time is wasted in rhetorical ornament, but every stroke tells upon the main point."

The Fisherman and His Friends.

A Companion Volume to "Christ and His Friends," consisting of Thirty-one Stirring Revival Discourses, full of Stimulus and Suggestion for Ministers, Bible class Teachers, and all Christian Workers and Others who Desire to become Proficient in the Supreme Capacity of Winning Souls to Christ. They furnish a rich store of fresh spiritual inspiration, their subjects being strong, stimulating, and novel in treatment, without being sensational or elaborate. They were originally preached by the author in a successful series of revival meetings, which resulted in many conversions. 12mo, Cloth, Gilt Top. Price, $1.50; post-free.

Bishop John F. Hurst: "It is a most valuable addition to our devotional literature."

New York Independent: "There is no more distinguished example of the modern people's preacher in the American pulpit to-day than Dr. Banks. *The volume fairly thrills and rocks with the force injected into its utterance.*"

Paul and His Friends.

A companion volume to "Christ and His Friends," "The Fisherman and His Friends," and "John and His Friends," being similarly bound and arranged. The book contains thirty-one stirring revival sermons delivered in a special series of revival services at the First M. E. Church, Cleveland. 12mo, Cloth, Gilt Top, Rough Edges. Price, $1.50.

Inter Ocean, Chicago: "The addresses are markedly practical, eloquent, earnest, and persuasive. Dr. Banks will especially interest the young. His illustrations are apt and pointed, and he gathers his facts from the wide range of literature past and present."

John and His Friends.

Thirty-three clear, straight, and forceful revival sermons, texts from the Gospel of John. They are of the same general character and excellence as the sermons contained in the three preceding volumes of this series. A companion volume to "Paul and His Friends," "The Fisherman and His Friends," and "Christ and His Friends." 12mo, Cloth, Gilt Top, Rough Edges, 297 pages. Cover Design in Gold, Bronze, and Black. Price, $1.50.

The Burlington Hawk-Eye, Burlington, Iowa: "A very gracious revival of religion was awakened by their delivery."

The Bookseller Newsdealer, and Stationer, New York: "Those who have read Dr. Banks's previous books need not be told that these sermons are original and practical and full of interesting illustrations and anecdotes."

Philadelphia Evening Item: "Revival literature has seldom if ever received so large a contribution from one man."

David and His Friends.

Thirty-one forceful revival sermons similar in general character to those in the preceding volumes of the "Friends" series. Texts from Samuel and the Psalms. A companion volume to "Christ and His Friends," etc. 12mo, Cloth, 320 pages, Gilt Top, Rough Edges. Price $1.50.

The Christian Guide, Louisville: "Will be sure of a hearty welcome from a multitude of preachers and religious workers who have found the preceding volumes so helpful and inspiring."

The Outlook, New York: "Evangelical, ethical, pointed with apt personal interest and narrative, every one of these sermons is a well-aimed arrow."

Chicago Times-Herald: "The sermons are not in the least orations, nor is their power in formal argument. It is rather in the power there is in statement and in pertinent illustration."

Hartford Courant: "These are the sort of sermons to be read at home, or even by a lay reader in the absence of the clergyman, for they are sufficiently graphic to dispense with a personal exponent."

The Christian Advocate, Detroit: "They are practical and are illustrated with everyday incidents. The author finds very striking subjects for his discourses."

BOOKS BY DR. LOUIS ALBERT BANKS — Continued.

On the Trail of Moses.

Thirty-one revival sermons revealing a wealth of suggestions and illustrations. 12mo, Cloth, gilt top, rough edges. $1.20.

Christian Index: "Dr. Banks has great facility in expressing themes that are pertinent to the lives people actually live, and his command of effective illustration is exceptional."

Lutheran Observer, Philadelphia: "One wonders at the variety of practical subjects all bearing on the every-day problems and needs of present-day life that he finds in the story of the great law-giver. The preacher will find in them a rich mine of illustrated material of a sort that really illumines."

The Unexpected Christ.

A series of thirty evangelistic sermons written in Dr. Banks's characteristic style. 12mo, Cloth, 328 pp. $1.50.

Bishop W. F. Mallalieu, D.D., LL.D.: "These sermons abound in hints, suggestions, and illustrations that will be helpful to the preacher."

Twentieth Century Knighthood.

Helpful addresses to young men in which examples of ancient chivalry are used to illustrate modern conditions. A companion volume to "The Christian Gentleman" and "My Young Man." 12mo, Cloth, 142 pp. 75 cents.

Herald and Presbyter, St. Louis: "It forms an irresistible appeal to young men to become, in very truth, twentieth century knights."

The Detroit Free Press: "The book abounds in pertinent anecdotes illustrating the virtues and beauties of a lofty Christian standard of manhood, and appeals to the highest and noblest qualities in young men, which may well be strengthened and developed by its perusal."

The Literary World, Boston: "Ten short practical appeals to the young men of the time to carry into modern life the instincts and principles which made chivalry what it was in the middle ages, with especial emphasis on sexual purity, temperance, and reverence for women."

Windows for Sermons.

A study of the art of sermonic illustration with 400 fresh illustrations suited for sermons and reform addresses. 12mo, Cloth, 440 pp. $1.20.

Western Presbyterian: "The illustrations should be worth many times the price of the book to the hard worked pastor."

Boston Journal: "This bulky volume contains a multitude of bright, practical ideas."

The Standard, Chicago: "The illustrations given are fresh, suggestive, and original, and will be found valuable to the preacher and lecturer."

Baltimore Methodist: "No minister of the gospel or other speaker on great moral problems will ever regret the purchase of this book."

BOOKS BY DR. LOUIS ALBERT BANKS—Continued.

Anecdotes and Morals.

Five hundred and fifty-nine attractive and forceful lessons which may be profitably utilized by the public speaker to freshly illustrate divine truth. They are almost entirely composed of incidents, happening throughout the world within the past few months. 12mo, Buckram, Gilt Top, Uncut Edges, 463 pages. Price, $1.50.

Boston Journal: "More than half a thousand anecdotes, some witty, all pointed and instructive, make up this unusual book. His anecdotes all have a purpose, and are prettily expressed."

The Globe-Democrat, St. Louis: "The index to the contents and the system of cross-references make the stories immediately available to whomever wishes to use them in illustration."

The Lutheran Observer, Lancaster, Pa.: "They are aptly related and always enforce the truths intended."

Herald and Presbyter, Cincinnati: "Altho there are so many selections, each new page contains some original lessons and a constant variety is maintained throughout."

The Christian Observer, Louisville, Ky.: "In this collection are found many anecdotes that are striking, well put, and in good taste."

Poetry and Morals.

Clear, straight, and forceful lessons emphasized by familiar passages of prose and poetry. The author has arranged several hundred simple truths in paragraphs appropriately headed in full-face type. The truths are explained in a few terse sentences, and then a verse, entire poem, or prose selection having direct bearing on the truth is added, forming a perfect storehouse of suggestive material for the preacher and writer. A companion volume to "Anecdotes and Morals." 12mo, Cloth, 399 Pages, $1.50.

A Year's Prayer-Meeting Talks.

Fifty-two suggestive and inspiring talks for prayer-meetings. Helpful material is provided for a whole year's weekly meetings. The talks have been already used by Dr. Banks in a most successful series of services. The author's well-known skill in presenting the old truths in bright and striking ways is evidenced in these interesting talks. The book is designed to be a right-hand aid for preachers and religious workers. 12mo, Cloth. Price $1.00.

Christian Work, New York: "The reader will be sure to be attracted and helped by such talks as these."

Baptist Outlook, Indianapolis: "Anecdotes, stories, bright similes, and poetical quotations enliven the talks."

Boston Times: "The subjects are treated in original ways, but never in a sensational or unwholesome manner."

www.ingramcontent.com/pod-product-compliance
Lightning Source LLC
Chambersburg PA
CBHW031426230426
43668CB00007B/447